The Wolf
from Scotland

The Wolf
from Scotland

The story of Robert Reid Kalley –
pioneer missionary

" Not I, but Christ "

W. B. Forsyth

Wenliscombe
11 - 2 - 89

EP

EVANGELICAL PRESS
12 Wooler Street, Darlington, Co. Durham, DL1 1RQ, England.
© Evangelical Press

First published 1988

ISBN 0 85234 256 X

British Library Cataloguing in Publication Data available.

Typeset by Outset Graphics, Hartlepool.
Printed in Great Britain by Anchor Press, Tiptree, Essex.

'Lord, thou knowest all my weakness, my folly, my sin, my utter inefficiency. But here I am. Oh, do thou take me, make me what thou wilt, send me where thou pleasest, do with me what thou seest fit, only let me feel thou art with me, that thou lovest me and employest me, and wilt be glorified by thy work done by thee through me!'

Dr Kalley's dedication after
his conversion

Dr Robert Reid Kalley

Contents

III Mission accomplished

Preface

I was asked by the Evangelical Fellowship of Congregational Churches to write a biography of Dr Robert Reid Kalley, pioneer missionary to Madeira and Brazil. In the latter country, under his inspired guidance, an indigenous church evolved, having a Brazilianized form of Congregational church polity and government. It was not imported from England or the States, but is as natural to Brazil as are the rain forests of the Amazon. For Dr Kalley that in itself was a considerable achievement.

Compiling this biography has been a labour of love, since I became one of a long line of spiritual and ecclesiastical 'heirs' to Dr Kalley's labours and travail. In Brazil I knew intimately some of the doctor's contemporaries: Pastor Fanstone, who laid the foundations of the Pernambucana Church in Recife; Dona Albertina, a step-daughter of the colporteur who took the gospel to Pernambuco, Vianna, and who, as a child, remembered sitting on Mrs Kalley's knee in Sunday School; Manoel de Souza Andrade, the elder statesman of the Pernambucana Church, who traced his spiritual roots to Dr Kalley's visit to Recife; the Braga family, son and grandson of the patriarch José Fernandes Braga. Much of what I know about Dr Kalley and his wife Sarah I learnt in conversation with these people.

I am debtor, also, to the writings of others – to Dr Michael P. Testa's *O Apóstolo de Madeira* and to the Rev. Manoel Porto Filho's manuscript, as yet unpublished, *O Apóstolo em Três Continentes – a Epopéia das Ilhas de Madeira*, both of these works in Portuguese, and exceedingly well documented. There will be those who feel that I should have quoted my sources in detail, as did these two eminent writers, but I am writing for people in general, and constant references and footnotes, while essential to the studious, can be a distraction, even an irritation, to the general reader. I append a bibliography.

I confess my indebtedness to the Canning Library, London, for lending me relevant books, not obtainable elsewhere, as also to the Fluminense Evangelical Congregational Church for giving me access to their extensive library. And, in this connection, I am especially indebted to the librarian, Dona Esther Monteiro, for her expertise and patience in making available to me the wealth of Kalley material in the library there.

When writing I have tried to bear in mind constantly that I am writing for British and not Brazilian readers, for those who, for the most part, are ignorant regarding Madeira and Brazil. The former is known as a tourist attraction, but to people in general even its location is unknown! Brazil, the largest of the Third World countries, with its multiple problems, is better known owing to the prominence given to it – and its misdeeds – in the media. To the general public, however, its past is shrouded in the mists of time; hence the frequent excursions into relevant historical events.

I confess to having succumbed to the temptation to introduce vignettes of the Madeiran and Brazilian co-workers with the Kalleys. Without their dedication and sacrifice the doctor and his wife could never have accomplished what they did. I feel that they would have wanted their life story to give full credit to these helpers.

It is impossible to narrate this chapter of the history of 'foreign missions' without reference to the persecution endured by the missionary couple and their converts. I write with a personal knowledge and experience of the violence resulting from such religious fanaticism – being taken into custody by the police, threatened with expulsion from the country as an 'undesirable', stoning, running the gauntlet through a hostile crowd, etc. – the whole gamut of persecution. The situation changed dramatically immediately after the Second Vatican Council, and since then by the whole-hearted endorsement by the Brazilian Roman

Catholic clergy of Liberation Theology. Protestants are no longer 'heretics'; they are 'separated brethren'.

Finally, may I add my sincere thanks to all those who have encouraged me to write and to complete this work, and in a very special way to my wife, Brenda, to whom I am indebted for her constructive comments, and for the arduous task of typing the manuscript.

W.B. Forsyth
Wiveliscombe.
December 1988

Introduction

Madeira and Brazil! What have they in common? Both were discovered and colonized by the Portuguese, and in accord with the dictates of Portuguese colonial policy, were Christianized also. In the sixteenth century they both formed part of Portugal's far-flung territories. There is also a close link in the history of missionary endeavour: Dr Robert Reid Kalley was the pioneer 'church-planter' both in Madeira and Brazil.

Dr Robert Reid Kalley (1809-1888) is unknown to most, even to those well-versed in mission history – a fact all the more surprising when many of his contemporaries on the mission field were men well-known and highly esteemed. William Carey went to India in 1793 and Robert Morrison to China in 1807. Adoniram Judson sailed for Burma in 1812 and John Williams for Polynesia in 1817. Robert Moffat left for Africa in 1816, followed by David Livingstone in 1841. These and many others were household names in church-mission circles, and were acclaimed nation-wide as men of outstanding achievement. Livingstone was buried in Westminster Abbey! Yet Dr Kalley, equally great, remained unknown, buried in a corner of a cemetery in Edinburgh which is very rarely visited, and what he accomplished on the mission field unrecognized even today.

Why? Several reasons may be adduced for this relegation to limbo, but among them two are of importance. First and foremost must be the fact that he did not go to what was considered to be a genuine mission field – a pagan land such as 'Darkest Africa' or India, China, Burma or the South Seas. These were heathen countries peopled by idolaters, followers of false cults, who walked in darkness and so were in dire need of the light of the gospel. In contrast, Madeira and Brazil, and similar Portuguese colonies, were deemed to be 'Christian', the domain of the 'Holy Mother Roman Catholic Church' and as such in no need of 'proselytizing Protestants'. A second reason why Dr Kalley remained unknown is that he did not represent any church or missionary society. He was an independent: he did not work under the auspices of any specific church, nor was he dependent on any missionary society for financial aid. He was a man of independent means – in the language of his day, a gentleman-missionary. He therefore lacked the publicity that a missionary society would have given him and, may it be said, he himself neither sought nor desired public recognition. In fact he shunned it.

And that leads us to a third factor – the character of the man himself. He was self-effacing, a man of a deep-seated humility. Like Moses of old, Dr Kalley was 'very meek', a lion when the interests of the Lord and his kingdom were at stake, but 'lowly and meek of heart' when interests of a purely personal nature were threatened. He was well known and greatly admired by a relatively limited circle of friends, but outside that circle he was unknown and his greatness went unrecognized.

Who, then, was Dr Robert Reid Kalley? The following is an attempt to make known the life and work of one of God's great pioneers and give him the honour which he merits.

Prologue

On the second Sunday in August 1846, a mass was held in the provincial capital of Madeira, Funchal, in honour of the patron saint, Our Lady of the Mount. It was an annual event, but this year excitement among her devotees was at fever pitch. The cathedral was packed, the crowd even spilling over into the square outside. From the pulpit a canon of the cathedral harangued the crowds, inciting them to violent action. The atmosphere was tense. There were excited murmurings, the venom of fanatical hatred, increasing in volume as the discourse drew to a close. The impatient multitude awaited the signal to act. Outside in the square that signal was given: a rocket swished into the air and exploded with a bang that could be heard all over town. Indeed its reverberations echoed all over the country. Madeira's 'St Bartholomew's Day' had come. Led by the canon, still in his priestly vestments, the crowd surged out into the Cathedral Square and on through the narrow streets leading to the suburb of Santa Luzia. Orchestrated slogans were chanted: 'Long live Our Lady of the Mount'; 'Death to the Calvinists'; 'Long live the Holy Mother Church'; 'Death to the Bible readers'; 'Death to Kalley – the Wolf from Scotland'.

What had Dr Kalley done to incur the wrath of the Catholic Church and the violence of the mob? There was nothing in his early life and upbringing to indicate how distinguished, and at times turbulent, his life would be.

1.
How it all began

Dr Kalley was born in Mount Florida, Glasgow, on 8 September 1809. He was the son of Robert Kalley, a wealthy and successful merchant, and his wife Jane Reid Kalley. His sister Jane had been born a year earlier. Both parents were members of the Church of Scotland, and in that church the infant Robert Reid was christened on 16 October 1809.

Before Robert was one year old his father died, and two years later his mother married David Kay, a widower with four children. A few years later, in 1815, Robert's mother died, but both Jane and Robert were well cared for in the home of their stepfather, the twice-widowed Mr Kay. They and the Kay children were a large, happy family. In later years Dr Kalley confessed the debt of gratitude he owed to his step-father: 'When I was young he was a true father to me: he persevered with me, giving me a moral and spiritual education by his example and his precepts – together with much prayer.'

Robert attended first the Rennie School and then the Glasgow Grammar School, and at the early age of sixteen was enrolled in an Arts Course at Glasgow University. His studies included rhetoric, advanced Latin and Greek – languages that would stand him in good stead in later life. Regarding his education he wrote, 'My education in early youth was with the intention of studying for the ministry in the Church of Scotland, as my grandfather was patron of the parish in which his estate lay, and the stipend of the minister was considerable (£350.*p.a.*) But, becoming an infidel on going to college I could not bear the thought of being obliged to preach that which I considered a parcel of lies. I therefore gave up all idea of becoming a clergyman and studied medicine.'

He entered the Pharmaceutical Laboratory attached to the Glasgow Royal Infirmary, receiving his diploma on 1 September 1827. Two years later he qualified in Pharmacy and Surgery at the Glasgow Faculty of Medicine and Surgery but it was only years later, in 1838, that he took his degree at the Glasgow University and became a 'Doctor in Medicine'.

His studies confirmed his unbelief. He later confessed that whether he looked through the microscope at wonders invisible to the naked eye, or gazed heavenwards through a telescope at the vastness of the universe, he could not see God! He did not believe in the existence of an eternal being, Creator and Sustainer of the universe. Of that period he wrote, 'I then thought that Christianity was all a delusion, and to make a confession of really believing it was enough to prove that a man must be either a fool or a knave.'

As a young graduate in 1829 he gained experience by serving as a ship's doctor on vessels plying between Glasgow, Bombay and the Far East. Little is known of the voyages he made but it is known that one of the ports of call was the island of Madeira. He wrote, 'That was on my way to the East Indies (1831)... and if I had been told then that I would be imprisoned there [in Funchal] for having distributed Bibles and teaching the doctrines they contain, I would have it as the most improbable thing that could be preconceived concerning me.'

A visit to Madeira was mere routine for seafarers, but for Dr Kalley it was to be something that would have a decisive influence in his life story. He was asked to sign on for yet another voyage, but he refused, fortunately, as it turned out, since the ship on which he would have sailed was lost in a storm with all hands. That was his second escape from death. He had narrowly escaped drowning as a boy when he was swimming with others in the River Clyde. On that occasion he got into difficulties and was rescued by a passer-by.

Steps towards faith

He begins to emerge from a sketchy background at the point

when he settled down as a medical practitioner in Kilmarnock, Ayrshire in 1832, where, in spite of his youth, he soon established for himself a reputation as a competent surgeon. Socially he was a success too. He was an extrovert and a lover of sport – very popular at parties. He earned for himself the sobriquet 'the dancing doctor of Kilmarnock'. He was still an atheist, blatant in his unbelief, but his early experiences as a doctor were to penetrate what he considered to be unassailable – his self-confession as an infidel. One patient made a lasting impression on him. The man, humble and poverty-stricken, yet rich in faith, witnessed to his doctor of the saving grace of Christ. There could be no doubt as to the man's sincerity and to the reality of his faith in Christ. A still greater impression was created by the testimony of another of his patients, a very poor woman dying of cancer. Her triumphant faith in the midst of so much misery and pain impressed the young doctor more than he cared to admit. She bore her trials of pain and poverty not merely with equanimity, but with joy! The room where she lay may have lacked even the barest necessities, but to the doctor when he made his frequent visits, it had an ethereal quality, something which his scientific mind could not explain. The risen Lord was making his presence and his glory a reality to his humble servant in the death throes of a wasting disease. Her witness shook the very foundations of Dr Kalley's unbelief. Could there be a God? 'Read the Book', she urged him; 'it's all in the Book!' Could Christ and his claims be true? He began to search the Scriptures diligently in an endeavour to discover the secret of her victory over the ravages of disease, the destitution of poverty and, ultimately, of death itself.

Faith did not come easily or dramatically; it developed slowly. He was helped towards it by a book, famous in its day, *Night Thoughts on Life, Death and Immortality* by Edward Young, L1.D. (1683-1765). This book was the outcome of tragedy and sorrow; the author had lost his wife and stepdaughter, leaving him desolate. Dr Kalley confesses that the 'Ninth Night', entitled 'Consolation', 'compelled me to confess the existence of something eternal'.

The text of this section of the book argues logically: 'What am I? And from whence? I know nothing but that I am; and since I am, conclude that I am something eternal.' Kalley's step-sister, Mary, a committed Christian, in correspondence with her brother, strongly recommended him to read the works of authors with a more evangelical outlook.

It was a book of a very different category that impelled him well on the way to a full-orbed faith – *Fulfilled Prophecy* by Dr Keith. Vestiges of doubt about the Christian faith, and a bemused attitude towards what he considered to be the credulity of professing Christians, still clouded his mind. 'But while reading the predictions regarding the Jews', he writes, 'and the literal fulfilment of them, that does look like a reasonable argument in favour of revelation.' This led to more intensive investigation of the prophecies, especially Deuteronomy, and then to an enquiry into other branches of Christian evidence, which resulted in the conviction 'that the infidel is more credulous than the Christian'.

Years later, in 1845, he addressed the General Assembly of the Free Church of Scotland in the following way: 'I was an infidel, and revelled in the coldness, the darkness, the thrill of openly declaring my unbelief. When I discovered, be it said to my satisfaction, that there is a God, and that this book [pointing to the Bible] is from God, I then felt that every Christian is called to enter that field of service in which he/she can use for God's glory the varied talents with which each has been endowed by God himself. As for me, I have had to think seriously in what way as a Christian doctor I can best serve the Son of God.'

Conversion and missionary call

The whole pattern of Dr Kalley's life changed. He became an active member of the Church of Scotland in 1833, being admitted to the communion. Not being content with merely belonging to a church, he took the initiative to help those most in need of aid. He gathered together a group of poor lads from his dispensary and taught them on Sunday and Thursday evenings. He dates his genuine conversion from this time (1834). The established church does not seem to have given him much encouragement, quite the contrary. A group of ministers condemned him 'for intruding into work to which he had no right when, as a Christian doctor, he assembled the poor and ignorant to teach the Scriptures to them'. Help was forthcoming, however, from ministers of churches, most of whom would subsequently leave the Establishment at the Disruption.

These were the years leading up to that Disruption. The Church of Scotland was in the throes of an acrimonious debate, principally on the matter of state interference and patronage versus a freer and more democratic form of church government, a debate which would culminate in a devastating schism. Several hundred clergy and laity, led by Dr Thomas Chalmers, walked out of the General Assembly to form the Free Church of Scotland. The situation was distressing and distasteful to the young convert. The whole experience was to influence his concept of church policy in later life.

At the same time, the foreign missionary movement was gathering pace. News of Robert Morrison's pioneering efforts to open China for the gospel thrilled the young doctor's evangelizing zeal. It would be about the time of his conversion that news of Morrison's lonely death in Canton reached Britain. What a worthwhile life! Morrison had succeeded in laying the foundations on which others would, and did, build, when China opened its doors to the preaching of the gospel eight years later. By 1818 Morrison had translated the Bible into Chinese and three years later produced a dictionary. These are the two corner-stones of missionary endeavour – the Bible and the language. If the situation in the Church of Scotland saddened Dr Kalley, the brighter prospects offered by service abroad attracted him.

In a magazine published by the London Missionary Society he read an appeal for medical missionaries. To him the appeal was personal and the call irresistible. One consideration was now paramount in his thinking, the insistent demand of the Lord himself: 'Go ye into all the world and preach the gospel', with the added promise: 'Lo, I am with you alway, even unto the ends of the earth, the end of the age, the end of the task.' Dr Kalley applied to the Church of Scotland Missionary Society for service in China. The Society expressed its regret: 'It does not appear to be right to enter any field of [missionary] work except one in which the Church of Scotland is already involved.'

Nothing daunted, he applied to the London Missionary

Society late in 1837. The L.M.S. was in urgent need of a medical missionary for China, making this application more than welcome. He made several journeys to London for interviews with the Board of Directors and was finally accepted for service in China. The Board minute of 7 November 1837 reads: 'Resolved that Dr Robert Reid Kalley of the Church of Scotland, Kilmarnock, recommended by the clergyman and by the Rev. John Ward, minister of the Congregational Church there, be accepted as assistant missionary and medical practitioner for China.' The Board gave him permission to stay in Scotland until 1839 'in order to improve his medical and theological knowledge'. He immediately sold his house and clinic in Kilmarnock to a Dr Miller, his future brother-in-law, and enrolled in Glasgow University to complete his studies in compliance with the wishes of the Society. Dr Miller, who married Jane Kalley, undertook to continue the classes for poor boys in Kilmarnock.

A door is closed

Then the hitch occurred. Dr Kalley became engaged to a young lady whom he had known for several years, and whose sterling Christian character and witness had impressed him even when he was an unbeliever. Her name was Miss Margareth Crawford, of Paisley. The doctor wrote to the L.M.S. enthusiastically about her – her dedication to Christ and to his cause; her aptitude for missionary work, an excellent education, practical experience as secretary to her father in his business; a happy, outgoing disposition; a lively interest in missions; a trained, disciplined mind that would enable her to write, to teach or to engage in other labours that the mission field might demand. There was, however, a serious drawback: her health was not robust. Her doctor, however, did give her a good report, stating that although not robust she had, since infancy, enjoyed remarkably good health. There was also another factor which Dr Kalley may not have taken into account seriously: she was brought up in very comfortable circumstances – not always the best preparation for the rigours of the mission field! Her minister too wrote an excellent testimonial: that she had been baptized by him as a child, had attended his classes for young people and, to quote, 'I have had good opportunities of ascertaining her abilities and character. She is possessed of highly respectable natural talents and from her youth has conducted herself with great propriety. She was early initiated into a knowledge of the Holy Scriptures and is evangelical in her sentiments and, I believe, decidedly pious. Her heart has, for some time, been set on missionary work, for which I consider her well qualified' (Paisley, 27.1.1838).

The L.M.S. was 'not amused'. The rules of the mission stipulated that no accepted candidate for missionary service could enter into any relationship with marriage in view without the express approval and permission of the Board. That ruling had been contravened. In correspondence with the mission Dr Kalley expressed his deep regret for any trouble or inconvenience his engagement may have caused and reimbursed the mission for any expense incurred by his application and acceptance. The L.M.S. had no alternative but to accept his resignation. The mission's minute, dated 30 January 1838, ends on a gracious note: 'If at any time he felt it his duty to serve on the mission field under the auspices of the L.M.S. due attention would be given to any request he might make.'

The *Glasgow Herald,* in its edition of 26 February 1838, carried the following announcement: 'Married at Oaksham House, Paisley, on 22nd instant, Robert R. Kalley, Esq. Surgeon, to Margareth, eldest daughter of the late John Crawford Esq. of Paisley.'

Another disturbing factor arose. Shortly before marriage Margareth had caught a chill which developed into pneumonia. It proved to be the beginning of tuberculosis, a malady with which she struggled bravely for the rest of her life. The door for missionary service in China was summarily closed, but Dr Kalley nurtured the hope that it would be for a short period only. However, China did benefit from his ministry. In January 1838 he was invited to speak at a meeting convened by the Church of Scotland Missionary Society, at which he spoke of the urgent need for the gospel to reach the Far East. As he spoke a young man felt the call to offer for missionary service. That young man was William Chalmers Burns who, in 1846, eventually reached China under the auspices of the English Presbyterian Missionary Society and blazed a trail in China for others to follow.

Part I
Madeira

2.
Arrival in Madeira

Dr Kalley, out of love and loyalty to his wife, gave her health priority. During the summer months it became evident that she must be spared the rigours of another Scottish winter. Her husband could think of no better climate for her than Madeira, that perfect gem of an island, 'the Pearl of the Atlantic', a 'floating garden' and an ideal place for recuperation after a severe illness. Indeed, a brochure of the time declares, 'Madeira is a resort for invalids of highly cultivated taste'! The high mountains protect the lee side of the island from the chilling north-east winds. The port of Funchal nestles in a natural amphitheatre at the foot of these mountains, a beautiful and magnificent setting for this, the capital city of the island.

In October 1838 the Kalleys set sail from Greenock for Funchal with the intention of wintering there. They were accompanied by Margareth's mother and her two sisters, one of whom was also ailing and in need of a more amenable climate. They had no thought of taking up permanent residence on the island, but neither did Dr Kalley think of accepting a post in Scotland. He had been offered an important position in Scotland, an offer that could have been taken up immediately following a few months convalescence in Madeira, but he declined the offer. China was still his ultimate goal, although for the immediate future it had to be Madeira. Little did the Kalleys know that they would spend a total of eight years on the island, still less that their ministry there would result in what Dr Andrew Bonar was to term 'the greatest happening in modern missions'.

The island of Madeira

Madeira was discovered by John Gonçalves Zarco in 1419, one of the intrepid mariners from the famous school of navigation in Sagres, Portugal, founded and supervised by Prince Henry the Navigator (1349-1460). Tradition holds that Prince Henry heard of the 'island paradise' in an extraordinary way. A legendary English couple, Robert and Ann, were thwarted in their budding romance by their parents. They decided to flee the country and embark for the continent. Storms blew them off course and eventually to the shores of Madeira. They had discovered a paradise, so great was the natural beauty: mountains, forests, flowers, birds. With the sailors they explored the hinterland but on returning to the coast, found that their boat had been carried away in a storm. The sailors began the arduous task of preparing some kind of craft that was seaworthy, but the romance of the young couple was short-lived. Both died within a short time of each other and were buried by the sailors at a site which is now the port of Machico. The crew finally put to sea, but were captured by Barbary pirates. One eventually escaped and reached Portugal. He informed Prince Henry of the discovery and as a result Zarco's expedition was mounted.

Zarco found no inhabitants on the island, only dense forests covering its volcanic mountain slopes. He gave it a descriptive name, Madeira – 'woodland'. Another of those early explorers had close links with Madeira. Christopher Columbus married into a Madeiran family and for some years lived there in Porto Santo.

The island's geographical position, on what would become the main shipping route from Europe to Central and South America, Africa and the Far East, made it of great strategical importance. It became an obligatory port of call for all shipping, the last opportunity for taking on supplies. At the turn of the nineteenth century as many as fifty or sixty vessels at a time could be found anchored in the sheltered harbour in the Bay of Funchal taking on fresh stores and water – wine as well.

The island to which the Kalleys were sailing was indeed foreign soil but with a strong British presence. Portugal is Britain's oldest ally, the alliance dating from the marriage of

Phillipa, daughter of John of Gaunt, to John, King of Portugal, in 1387. In the nineteenth century Madeira was undoubtedly a 'commercial colony' of Britain; a century earlier it had almost become a British colony *de facto*! When Charles II married Catherine of Bragança, a Portuguese princess, in 1662, he received as a dowry £500,000 together with Tangier and – of greater importance to Britain – the island of Bombay, a foundation stone of the Indian Empire. Records show that Madeira was also considered for inclusion in the dowry! Had it been so it would have been a valuable addition to Britain's colonies.

Soon after Funchal was founded in 1508 Britain had forged strong commercial links with Madeira. By the eighteenth century the English Factory, a corporation of British business men, had become the most powerful factor in the economy of Madeira. It dominated the island's trade – sugar, wine, textiles, embroidery, wicker-work, chandlery and shipping in general. It almost constituted a state within a state, with its own club, church, chaplains, doctors, hospital wards, cemetery, and its charities including pensions for needy expatriates, together with free medical treatment and burial. The English Factory was very exclusive. No one could become a member of the corporation 'unless he had an uninterrupted, respectable commercial establishment for not less than six years'! During the Napoleonic Wars the strategic importance of Madeira was so vital to British interests, and especially to the Navy, that a British military force, several thousand strong, occupied the island as a precautionary measure, first in 1801-1802 and later from 1808-1814, when Napoleon invaded the Iberian Peninsula.

The Kalleys arrive in Madeira

To Dr Kalley the entrance to Funchal was already well known, but to his wife and her family it must have been a thrilling experience. A contemporary writer describes it graphically: 'The approach to Madeira by sea was dramatic. After the ship rounded the Cape of Garajua, the vista of the city of Funchal gradually unfolded. The white spots grew larger until one could distinguish them as houses. Those of the wealthy with towers used for sighting ships, and upper stories with grilles, easily distinguishable from the poorer houses of the people. Much higher, almost at the summit of the Mount, could be seen, amid the foliage of the trees, the two white towers of the Church of Our Lady of the Mount... to the west, the warlike Spanish fort, the Pico Fort (1632) ... to the east, the Fort of Santiago ... straight in front, behind the pebble beach, the edifice São Lourenco, a hotch-potch of architectural styles which served the multiple purpose of a palace, a fortress, a barracks and the residence of the governor ... in the very centre of the beach, something unique, the Pillar of Banger, a column built by an Englishman, John Light Banger (1726-1798), to secure the mooring ropes of merchant vessels.' All this, against a background of majestic beauty – the towering mountains of central Madeira. There was no quay for berthing; ships rode at anchor in the bay. The Kalleys would be transferred from the ship to small boats, rowed ashore and then carried through the shallows to the beach by porters.

On landing they would have found themselves members of a considerable colony of their fellow-countrymen – residents, convalescents, tourists – a British enclave in foreign but very pleasant surroundings. The houses, shops and buildings generally gave the town a genuine Portuguese flavour. Steep, cobbled streets, generally narrow, but a few a little wider, opened up into *praças*, squares, and occasionally into *alamedas*, tree-lined avenues. With its evenly temperate climate all the year round and its pleasing appearance, Funchal was an ideal place in which to live, even for a short stay. The Kalleys and Crawfords rented a house, set in ample grounds, in the Vale Formoso, overlooking the town of Funchal.

Since there were so many invalids and convalescents in the British community, possibly as many as 300, Dr Kalley found himself pressed into service. He was soon fully occupied giving them medical advice and treatment, and, as a committed Christian, was constrained to deal with their souls too. His gifts as a personal evangelist were put to good use. The Church of England was already well established in Funchal and for long decades had held regular services for British subjects. The church building was of more recent construction, having been built by the British Factory in 1822, and was

The cathedral in Funchal – mid eighteenth century

remarkable for its style of architecture. Portuguese law prohibited a Protestant church from having the external appearance of an ecclesiastical building. The church was, therefore, circular, a style formerly adopted by the Knights Templar. There was a chaplain too, a Mr Lowe. As for the Presbyterian Scots, they paid a perfunctory tribute to the Sabbath and the kirk and thought that nothing further was required of them. For most of them the strict Sabbath observance such as they had known in Scotland no longer applied to life in Madeira. To the doctor such an attitude was the outward sign of an inward malady. He was a strict observer of the Sabbath but from a right motive. For him the day was not a meaningless, irksome burden, a yoke to be thrown off as soon as circumstances might permit; rather it was the Lord's Day. As such it was a day to be kept holy, separate, sanctified; a day for worship in God's house with God's people; a day of rest and renewal when the ordinary daily routine was suspended or reduced to a minimum. It was not the rules of the Kirk Session, nor yet the dictates of contemporary society that orientated Dr Kalley, but obedience and loyalty to the Lord who sanctified the day.

The first Sunday in Funchal the doctor attended the service in the Anglican Church, but he found worship so formal and deadening to the soul that he resolved never to return there. The following Sunday he conducted worship in his own home for the family and Portuguese servants. He soon discovered among his fellow-countrymen a few who were desirous of meeting together for Bible study and prayer, and as a result, early in December, informal services in the Scottish tradition began to be held in a private house.

3.
The call of God

Dr Kalley was a gifted personal evangelist; he could talk to a person in a quiet, gracious, informal way and hold his or her attention without causing embarrassment or arousing animosity. Yet in Madeira he was anxious to do more than just converse with individuals on a personal basis; he wanted to conduct services also. In this he found himself at a considerable disadvantage. He relived his experiences in Kilmarnock when ministers and elders of the established kirk had questioned his right to engage in religious activities – teaching, preaching and conducting services – matters they considered outside the confines of his medical profession. Foremost in his condemnation of Dr Kalley's initiative to reach his fellow-countrymen resident on the island of Madeira was the Anglican chaplain. He warned people against a man who did not believe in baptismal regeneration and who taught the Bible to the exclusion of the Prayer Book! Considerable correspondence exists, written at that period, which reveals Dr Kalley's dilemma. Should he seek ordination? Would that tie him to a particular church and so hamper his freedom? These and other cogitations give a vivid insight into his personality, not least his assertive independent spirit.

Ordination to the ministry

On 30 January 1839 Dr Kalley wrote from Madeira: 'It will be my duty to lift up a standard for the truth. I would willingly do so at once ... for I do not regard the licence from any body of men at all *essential* before preaching the glad tidings of salvation to perishing souls. The message is God's, not man's, and the licence required is therefore licence from God and this appears to me so plainly given in his Word that I would have no hesitation on that score. But, such are the views and feelings of my countrymen that few would attend unless I were formally set apart ... as I would be exceedingly averse to do anything to mar my own usefulness, I would become all things to all men if I might gain some – as well as considering ordination desirable though not essential to preaching, and as it would be desirable to be empowered to administer baptism and the Lord's Supper – which with my present views I would not feel authorized to do as a layman, I would willingly go to England in the spring, remain in a course of study if required, if I might get ordination and return to this place ... As to the body of Christians from whom I would desire ordination, I consider that of little moment, if they hold the great essentials of the truth and will allow me freedom to be guided by my own views on God's Word in minor matters.'

The following day he wrote to the London Missionary Society. The minute of the Candidates' Committee of the L.M.S. dated 25 March 1839 reads: 'A letter was read from Dr R.R. Kalley, M.D., with the date of 1st February 1839 from Funchal, in which he offers his services as an agent of this Society, to work in Madeira, should the members of the Committee consider that place to be within their sphere of service; requesting further that he be ordained as a preacher of the gospel, both to his own fellow-countrymen as also to the Portuguese residents on the island. Resolved: Recommend to the Board that in accordance with the considered opinion of this committee, seeing that Madeira is not within the sphere of the work of this Society, the offer should not be accepted. It was decided also that since certain members of the committee are ready, in the exercise of their own personal authority, to ordain Dr Kalley as a preacher of the gospel of Christ, that he be informed of this decision immediately, in order that he might come to London for that purpose.'

The suggestion was made to Dr Kalley, undoubtedly by his Scottish friends in Madeira, that he apply to the Church of Scotland for ordination. Dr Kalley did not agree with the suggestion since it would mean a long delay. To quote, 'Presbyterianism required some three or four years of theological study, and this was out of the question since the King's business requires haste.' He added that 'Madeira was alive and stretching forth her hands for the gospel.' Prolonged absence from Madeira was unthinkable. Episcopal ordination was suggested as an alternative, but Dr Kalley's strong Presbyterian convictions precluded such a thing. On a fragment of paper which survived the bonfire lit by his persecutors in Funchal in 1842, he expresses these convictions: 'Without further detention it may suffice to say that the views I entertain are those of the standard Church of Scotland, and with regard to baptism and the Lord's Supper I coincide with them.' This fragment proved to be the final paragraph of a Confession of Faith Dr Kalley had prepared for his ordination in 1839.

On 5 April 1839 the Rev. John Arundel, secretary of the L.M.S., wrote to Dr Kalley in Madeira: 'Several individual ministers in London, members of the Society [L.M.S.] would have no objection whatever in their individual capacity to unite in your ordination, viz. Dr Henderson, Dr Rood ... etc. I must, therefore, leave to your decision whether you will avail yourself of this offer and at what time. I shall be happy to render you all possible assistance in getting the meeting, and applying to the different parties to be engaged. Indeed, my own place of worship I most readily tender for the service, and when I hear from you as to the time of your coming I will instantly proceed with the necessary arrangements: of course, not as a member of the Society, but as one of the ministers of Christ in the metropolis who knows you and esteems you and will be ready to do all that he can to promote the important object contemplated.'

Later, Dr Kalley wrote, 'There was a deeply interesting field opening to me and it was very precious in such circumstances to have a company of pastors in the fold of Christ – some of whom had grown old in his service – to pray with me and for me, laying their hands on my head and bidding me "God speed" in the service of the Lord. It was cheering and comforting to have men in the service of the Lord agreeing to recognize in me those gifts which I believe God to have conferred on me for his own service. This was my motive in going to London. My desire was that those taking part in this solemn work should be men of God whose labours had been successful in inducing sinners to confide in the Messiah Jesus. I had met with some such men in London, and cared little about the denomination of the party or parties with which they were associated – provided that they would unite in that which I desired, and leave me unbound to party, so that there might be no interruption of those catholic views and feelings in which I delight. I wish to feel still that all who truly believe in the Lord Jesus are living members of one glorious body, and that no form of ordination nor any views about church government ought to separate, or really could separate me, from any such men. I did not wish to appear to separate myself from them by joining a party, while I earnestly desired the affectionate "God-speed-you" of his faithful servants.'

Yet again he writes, 'In Madeira I assured the people, as was most true, that what I did was entirely of my own accord, and unconnected with any church and unemployed by any party.' Also, 'I am grieved by the evils of sectarianism and remain unconnected with any one sect or party of Christians more than with another.' At the Disruption, although he sympathized whole-heartedly with the seceders, he refused to join them as, in his view, to have done so would have compromised his rugged independence.

On 1 June 1839 he left Madeira *en route* for London via Lisbon. He had already applied for a Portuguese medical diploma which would enable him to treat Madeirans, and not merely his fellow-countrymen. Having passed the official examination and received his diploma from the *Escola Médica Cirúrgica de Lisboa* on 17 June, he continued his journey to London, arriving there on 1 July. He was ordained, or as he himself preferred to call it 'recognized', on 18 July in Dr Bennet's Chapel in Silver Street, London. During his brief visit he sought 'to get all possible insight into systems of teaching and to hear the most popular preachers, to fit myself for the duties which probably awaited me on returning'. He confessed also to having been 'very moved by the religious excitement in Kilsyth', a town from which, through the ministry of William Chalmers Burns, the breath of revival spread throughout the Central Highlands.

The plight of Madeira

What did Dr Kalley mean when he declared, 'Madeira is alive, stretching forth her hands for the gospel,' and that while in Britain he 'endeavoured to fit myself more for the duties that probably await me on returning to Madeira'? Obviously he envisaged that on his return from the ordination ceremony his ministry would widen considerably and that it would extend far beyond the limitations of the British colony. The British colony in Madeira, like similar British enclaves elsewhere overseas, was very gregarious and insular. It sought to conserve the British way of life even in a foreign culture. The 'town club' and the 'country club' with its bar and recreations – cricket, football, tennis – were equally exclusive. The church, too, whether episcopal or Presbyterian, with its services in English, its own chaplain or ministers, its religious inbreeding, was all exclusively British and utterly void of missionary vision. Contact with the 'natives', the Madeirans, was kept to a minimum – strictly business and only, in exceptional circumstances, social. Most of the British did not even trouble to learn the language of the host country. There was one contact, however, that could not be avoided, the servants. Every household had its domestic staff, 'natives', and the relationship of master and servant had to exist.

The Kalleys too had their domestics, Madeirans of the peasant class. To them these servants were not merely chattels, ignorant, stupid, a necessary evil and a convenient topic for conversation over tea! To them they were human beings and should be treated as such. Dr Kalley, with his knowledge of Latin, easily learned their language, Portuguese, and he began to communicate with them and understand their needs. He was appalled at their ignorance and superstition. None of them knew how to read or write, and as to their religion, it had degenerated into Christianized paganism. On his return to Madeira Dr Kalley was ready to act.

The plight of the Madeirans was indeed desperate in every way. It was a time of economic recession. The sugar industry, once the mainstay of the island's economy, was in decline. The vineyards, already world-famous for the excellency of the wine they produced, were unable to cope with the situation alone. The authorities in Lisbon prohibited the manufacture of goods on the island; all manufactured goods had to be imported. Embroidery and wicker-work had not yet come into their own. The peasants eked out an existence cultivating the terraces clinging to the precipitous mountain flanks. The few who were fortunate enough to possess a cow could not turn it out to graze, an impossibility on such steep hillsides, but had to keep it tethered in a hut. Life was hard for these peasants. They lived in isolation even from each other. There were no roads; trails wound their way on the dangerously steep mountainsides, usually following the *levadas,* or irrigation channels. Poverty abounded, as did the ills associated with it, ignorance and disease. Such grinding poverty deeply moved Dr Kalley, but even more so the absolute dearth of genuine religion. The immediacy of the need constituted his call to missionary service in Madeira.

Madeira, like the Azores, had been uninhabited when the Portuguese discovered it. They colonized it and took with them their own particular brand of Roman Catholicism. Basically it differed from medieval Catholicism in the rest of Europe. The Moors, during the centuries in which they dominated the Iberian Peninsula, introduced a streak of fatalism into popular religion. In a time of crisis the Portuguese shrugged their shoulders and resigned themselves to their fate, with the attitude: '*Deus assim quer*' – 'God wants it to be so.'

Roman Catholicism also claimed Madeira as its exclusive domain. All other branches of Christianity were considered heretical and consequently banned. To substantiate such a claim, in 1554, immediately after the Portuguese occupation, the cathedral in Funchal was built, the first cathedral to be built outside mainland Portugal.

In practical terms the highlights of religion were not the mass and the confession, important as these might be, but saints' days. On such days the atmosphere was that of a carnival: the saint carried shoulder-high in procession, houses decorated for the occasion, flowers strewn in the way, best clothes and feasting. A perfunctory acknowledgement was paid to the saint by holding a mass, with the women crowding inside the church and the men congregating outside. The mass over, festivities began in earnest. The saint was forgotten and the sensuous prevailed. Religion was a blending of ignorance, superstition and credulity. Biblical Christianity was unknown.

In Dr Kalley's soul the fire of the gospel burned. He was ready to act on his return to Funchal in October 1839, qualified as a doctor in Portuguese territory and ordained as a minister of the gospel, and act he did. The poor were entirely without medical assistance, so he would use a medical ministry not only to meet that need but also to serve as a stepping stone to his ultimate goal – the preaching of Christ to the poor. He would treat their bodily ailments but he would meet their souls' need too. He wrote in his diary, 'I am occupied during the whole afternoon and evening, from 3 to 9 o'clock, with just one hour free to take tea and hold family worship, but the joy of this work is all the greater.' Years later he was to tell the General Assembly of the Free Church of Scotland: 'I confess that I find it strange to be on a small island in the middle of the ocean instead of going where I thought my sphere of Christian service would be – China. However, I can say, "Use me, Father, as best may seem in your sight."'

4.
Seed-time and harvest

Medical work

The Kalleys had settled in the Santa Luzia district of Funchal, not far from the palatial home of the leading English resident on the island, Henry Veitch, the 'consul-general'. It was there in the Caminho do Monte, the following year, that he opened a clinic which he later amplified into a 'cottage' hospital with twelve beds. He speedily gained fame as a doctor on the island, even the Roman Catholic bishop becoming his patient. He treated both rich and poor. As he himself confessed, his fees for the rich were very high, but this served a dual purpose: it discouraged the wealthy from seeking his professional assistance – there were two other British doctors in town – and this left him with more time to attend to the poor; it also provided him with extra funds to finance the treatment of his poorer patients. These he treated gratis: free consultations, free medicine and, if hospitalization was necessary, that was free too. On an average he treated some fifty patients a day, many of whom were carried to his clinic in hammocks slung on a pole between two bearers, and not infrequently they had travelled over rough, precipitous mountain tracks. Many on arrival were too ill to respond to treatment. Even his young sister-in-law died of tuberculosis at that time in spite of all the expert medical attention he could give her.

Dr Kalley was a skilled physician, but essentially he was a missionary. As he had planned, his medical ability proved to be the means for the furtherance of the gospel. He was steadfast and fearless in his witness, as is shown by his custom of kneeling at the bedside of a patient, when called to treat a sick person at home, to ask God's guidance in the treatment and his blessing on all present. He had a Scripture verse printed on each prescription, and in the clinic he insisted that patients attend morning prayers, which comprised a short Scripture reading, a brief exposition and prayer. The result of such a ministry was predictable. The poor had never had anyone who cared for them, and here was one who 'sat where they sat', who came down to their level, entered into their experience of poverty, oppression and hardship, one to whom Madeirans were brothers. A wave of gratitude to the *santo ingles* – the 'English saint' – spread over the island. He was acclaimed as the 'good doctor'. Interest in the gospel was aroused: people wanted to know about the good news. They were seeing its powerful witness in the life of this *bom doutor*.

Even priests were numbered among his patients, some of whom became very friendly. Naturally he conversed with them on spiritual matters, but was careful to avoid controversial subjects such as saints, the mass, purgatory, transubstantiation, confession and the like. He adopted a positive attitude, and restricted conversation to the basic essentials of the gospel – the person of Christ, the efficacy of his saving work on the cross, the faith that leads to salvation and the essential holiness and love in the Christian life. One priest journeyed from Seixal on the northern coast to discover for himself the secret of the doctor's success with such ignorant folk as the peasant class – he had made them understand gospel truth.

A gracious leader

At one point, when the doctor's health was adversely affected by the strain of such intense activity, his friends persuaded him to take a 'rest' away in the mountains, some six hours' journey from Funchal. News quickly spread as to where he was and people began to gather. At one point, in a place called São Jorge, 1500 came to hear him expound the Scriptures. An interesting sidelight is that the local parish priest boldly announced the meeting from the pulpit and gave the doctor his unrestricted co-operation! Later, when the priest was accused of collaborating with the 'heretical foreigner', he defended himself by stating that 'Far from Dr Kalley having spoken anything offensive or illegal on that occasion, he had read extensively from the Holy Bible, and had said nothing against what the Holy Apostolic Roman Catholic Church teaches us to believe.' The 'good doctor' was not an intolerant bigot. If a patient in the hospital wanted a visit from the priest, permission was given instantly.

He did not neglect his own fellow-countrymen, but conducted regular, if informal, services for them. In the absence of a Church of Scotland minister he, as an ordained minister, presided at the biennial celebration of the Lord's Supper.

The doctor was a forceful yet gracious personality. His build and his dignified bearing made him a natural leader. He was a true Scot, canny, ruggedly independent, resolute in action and honest in all his dealings. His faith was straightforward and uncluttered, fashioned not in the halls of theological colleges, but in the practical issues of everyday life. His teacher had been the Holy Spirit and his text-book the Bible. And he was a good pupil: he had an ordered and disciplined mind, which enabled him to grasp and to hold fast revealed truth. His articles of faith, adhered to down through the years, testify to this.

He was a pragmatist in the philosophical sense: the truths in which he ardently believed must be put to the test through his contacts with his fellow men. Through the Word the living Christ had granted to him a new life and purpose; similarly he expected others to experience this too. They too must be born again.

As a committed Christian he was richly endowed with the graces of his Master – meekness and humility. In utter self-denial he obeyed the Scripture injunction to 'look not only to his own interest but also on the interests of others'.

Even his gratuitous 'enemies' testified to his greatness. One of the most illustrious, Padre Fernando Augusto da Silva, wrote in the *Ilucidário Madeirense*: 'He was a man of extraordinary talent and a notable physician-surgeon, possessing the rare gift of swaying multitudes with his suggestive and eloquent discourses, and this was the secret of the effectiveness of his (religious) propaganda ... He was, without doubt, a true believer, but over and above all, he was also a fanatic. At first he limited his activities to free medicine, and in that way became notable for his charity towards the poor, and to the founding of free schools. That, together with his attractive personality and his influential words, resulted in the creation round his name of an aura of sympathy, esteem and respect on the part of all classes of society.'

A Brazilian biographer, Dr Manoel Porto Filho, draws a comparison between Dr Kalley and John Robinson. The latter was a leader of the Puritan Separatists, first in Scrooby Manor, afterwards in Leyden, Holland, and is best known as pastor of the *Mayflower* emigrants for conscience' sake. Both men sought to exercise a conciliatory ministry characterized by a genteel courtesy, a spirit of understanding, that sought to avoid confrontations or polemics.

In Funchal Dr Kalley even visited the Roman Catholic bishop in his palace in an endeavour to make his motives and aims clear. He conversed freely with the more tolerant among the Roman Catholic priests, avoiding futile arguments. He had great facility in communicating divine truth in language easily understood. Further, he elucidated the gospel with imagery drawn from everyday life. He also possessed that rare gift when dealing with someone, of whatever social status, of giving his whole attention to that person; it was as if no one else existed, and the poor loved it.

He has left on record a self-portrait, incomplete but revealing: 'You may desire to know something about the writer! He is [in 1846] about thirty-seven years of age, with a bald head and black whiskers, in height about 5'10"; not at all of a melancholy countenance; not very particular in his dress but generally in black.'

Schools for the people

Motivated by the desire to teach adults to read the Bible, he opened his first school before the end of 1839. The Bible had been central to his conversion, and it was central to his personal life and witness. It would be the corner-stone of his educational policy, in the belief that as the Holy Spirit had unfolded its truths to him, so he would do the same for the unlettered peasants as they learned to read its sacred page. The network of schools spread over all the countryside.

Madeira had never had free state schools and as a result only the upper classes received any education, which was rudimentary at best. Higher education could only be found in schools on the Portuguese mainland. On the island itself education left much to be desired. The eldest son was sent to the priests' school to be taught and the remainder of the family were reduced to picking up any knowledge they could glean from the favoured eldest brother. Dr Kalley opened school after school for the poor who had previously been condemned to be kept in ignorance. He provided the teachers, furnishings and teaching materials. School was free for the children by day and for adults at night. The school houses were primitive, usually in a room in a cottage. Pupils were drawn from the immediate neighbourhood, but at night men came after a heavy day's work in the fields, often walking great distances, all eager to learn to read. The teachers only had the bare basics of education but, motivated by Dr Kalley's enthusiasm, they dedicated themselves to the task of helping their neighbours. Any remuneration they may have received came from the doctor himself, but it had to be relatively insignificant. In spite of every difficulty the schools progressed and gradually, as pupils learned to read, the system of each-one-teach-one evolved, a century before Dr Laubach introduced this method of teaching world-wide. As soon as someone learned to read he perfected his ability by teaching someone else. Shortly there were some twenty schools established with 800 pupils. Two books were used: the Portuguese 'ABC' and the Bible.

Regarding these schools a fellow-countryman wrote, 'I attended the examination of some of the scholars and to me it was a source of wonder how advanced they were in their studies and, incidentally, how grateful they were to Dr Kalley for the teaching they were receiving. I do not think that I am exaggerating in affirming that several hundred learnt much in a very short space of time. Before, they were as stupid as the donkeys they drove, but now in contrast they were intelligent readers of the Bible.'

To quote from a letter written by Dr Kalley, 'Hundreds of men, after heavy labours in the fields, went to school at night, and in almost every case they were motivated by the desire not merely to read the words of men, but the Word of God. I think that almost two and a half thousand attended these schools between 1839 and 1845 and that well over a thousand between the ages of 15 and 30 learned to read the Scriptures intelligently, and to study them for themselves.' The Bible was the text-book and during these years 3000 copies of the Bible were distributed in the schools and among the population in general. These were the only copies of the Bible in Madeira, except for some eighty volumes for the use of the clergy, sent in 1842 at the express wish of D. Maria II, Queen of Portugal. She admonished the priests to read the Bible for their own edification and for that of their flock in Madeira!

In his letter Dr Kalley adds: 'In 1839 a few showed a great desire to read and to hear the Word of God. In 1840 this interest grew somewhat and many adults went to school because they wished to learn to read the Bible. In 1841 interest grew even more. The following year, especially during the summer and autumn, people flocked in large numbers to hear the Scriptures read and explained.'

Naturally, all this activity attracted the attention of the authorities, but popular opinion was so much on the side of the doctor, that they hesitated to act. Like the chief priests of old, 'they feared the people'. Of those early days Dr Kalley wrote: 'In the beginning of my intercourse with the Madeirans I met few of them who had ever seen a Bible or seemed to know that the New Testament was written by men who went about with the Lord Jesus Christ when he dwelt on earth. When one part of it was shown to them as the work of Peter, another as that of John, and a third as that of Matthew, some doubted and wanted proof. Others listened, with eager attention, while a portion of it was read to them as a specimen of the contents.'

Dr Kalley, amongst his varied talents, possessed the gift of writing hymns. He composed a number of hymns and taught the people to sing them. As literacy increased he wrote a number of tracts and pamphlets. Before he left the island he had translated into Portuguese Bunyan's *Pilgrim's Progress,* possibly some of it while in prison when, like Bunyan himself, 'I walked through the wilderness of this world, I lighted on a certain place where was a den and laid me down in that place to sleep...'

Stirring days

These stirring days are described by one who lived through them: 'In 1842, especially in the summer and autumn, people came in large numbers to have the Scriptures read and explained to them, many people walking ten or twelve hours, and climbing over mountains three thousand feet high! The meetings were solemn, the hearers listened with unwearied attention, a hand was observed stealing to remove a tear, and sometimes there was a general audible expression of wonder. This was especially the case when the subject of the remark was the love of God, in not sparing his own Son, but giving him up to die for the sins of the whole world, and the love of Christ in voluntarily taking upon himself the wrath and curse we deserved. For several months, I believe, there were not fewer than a thousand people present each Sabbath: generally they exceeded two thousand, occasionally reached three thousand and, at least on one occasion were reckoned at five thousand. On the last-mentioned occasion seventy New Testaments were sold, and many intending purchasers were disappointed. These meetings were in the open air. You may well imagine the interest awakened by such a scene in a popish country!'

'In some places the general topics of everyday conversation, when walking along the roads, or resting a little from labour in the fields, were the Word of God, the love of the Lord Jesus Christ, the peace of God, the hope of glory, the folly of image worship, the uselessness of penance. Often, too, the hymns of the Sabbath were heard through the week among the fields and vineyards, and there was much searching of the Scriptures to know the Lord's declaration on subjects brought before them.'

Dr Kalley explains how this awakening was brought about in those early days. 'Gratuitous medical aid induced many to visit us and experience the benefits which they prized. It led them to regard me as a friend. When conversing with them about the diseases of their bodies and the remedies which they were to employ, it required little effort to turn their attention to the disease of the soul, the Physician, the remedy and the results: and thus they listened with less prejudice than they would have done in other circumstances.'

The Edinburgh Medical Mission places on record that Dr Kalley's success as a medical missionary was unsurpassed in any other mission field. Such skill as a doctor, such perception as an educator, such power as a preacher and such faithfulness and resourcefulness as a personal evangelist could only result in the mighty power of God being unleashed.

5.
The gathering storm

Madeira was not only 'stretching forth her hands for the gospel' but now filling those hands with the gospel. Such outstanding success in the preaching of the gospel could not go unchallenged. The storm-clouds gathered on the horizon and rapidly darkened, to burst finally with savage ferocity over the nascent Madeiran church. So fierce and concentrated was the persecution that Madeira was equated with Madagascar, that other island where satanic savagery decimated the church.

A public testimonial

On 25 May 1841 an expression of gratitude to Dr Kalley for his philanthropic efforts on behalf of the poor, sick and uneducated, was registered in the minutes of a meeting of the municipal council in Funchal. The minute, translated from the Portuguese, reads: 'This Chamber has been informed through the Administrator of the Council, in an official document dated today, that Robert Reid Kalley, British citizen and Doctor of Medicine, has continuously occupied himself with the highest of high philanthropy: maintaining at his own expense primary schools in the various parishes of this council and district; prescribing and ministering medicines free of any charge to people who come to him; maintaining also, with his own money, next to his home, a hospital where there are always to be found interned several patients; explaining to the people who wish to listen to him the text of the Holy Scriptures of the gospel, without taking part in any polemics that

The Bay of Funchal – mid eighteenth century

might damage in some way the dogmas and disciplines of the Catholic Church; exhorting all as to the necessity of fulfilling the moral demands of their religion:

'– resolved that honourable mention be made of all these benefactions from this Chamber and in the name of the Municipality which it represents, a copy of this minute be sent to the said Dr Kalley as an expression of public gratitude to him.'

Growing pressures

Even as gratitude was being expressed publicly, protests at the doctor's missionary outreach were growing. The Bishop of Madeira, who was not only a patient of 'the good doctor' but also a personal friend, warned him that a letter had been received from Lisbon urging that 'activity in the medical and educational spheres that was endangering law and order be curtailed'. That, of course, referred to Dr Kalley! The letter may well have included a decree promulgated by the Roman Catholic Church in Portugal:

'Anyone failing to respect the religion of the kingdom, the Roman Catholic Apostolic Church, shall be condemned to imprisonment for one to three years, and a fine proportional to his income, in each of the following cases:
1   Injuring the said religion publicly, in any dogma, act or object of worship, by deed or word or publication in any form;
2   Attempting by the same means to propagate doctrines contrary to the Catholic dogmas defined by the Church;
3   Attempting by any means to make proselytes, or conversions to a different religion or sect condemned by the Church;
4   Celebrating public acts of worship, not that of the Catholic faith at which Portuguese citizens are present.'

Further opposition arose from the Portuguese doctors in Funchal. They did all in their power to discredit *o bom doutor inglês*. Professionally they could not fault him, but they declared that his philanthropy in the spheres of medicine and education were a mere cover-up: his true intention was to propagate his religion and undermine popular support for the state religion. He was a perverting element.

There was difficulty too with the importation of Bibles

from the Bible Society in London. A consignment was retained in customs. Miraculously the Queen of Portugal herself intervened and ordered that the Bibles be released at once, severely reprimanding those who sought to restrict the beneficent activities of the *médico inglês*!

The bishop and the judge

The doctor was not without friends who sought to defend him. A number of the more moderate clergy with whom Dr Kalley had been friendly prepared a document, signed by them all, defending him against these accusations. The vicar-general took the document to the doctor for his comment and appreciation. It had been badly written and much of it was couched in language of which he could not approve. One statement was definitely not true – that the doctor preached the same message preached by the clergy from their pulpits! He and the vicar-general attempted to rewrite it, but without success. Mrs Margareth Kalley wrote in her diary, 'Robert thinks that the document should not be signed or sent. He and the vicar are attempting to rewrite it. I think that the time for the free propagation of the gospel is coming to an end.' The doctor sent to the bishop a copy of the Bible he was distributing. The bishop replied, 'My dear friend and sir: God, our good Father often permits that we should be persecuted by our enemies, in order that, after our patience has been put to the test with sufferings, we may triumph over their machinations. He will save us, because he is all-powerful, great and just. I received the copy of the Scriptures and am much obliged. Your friend, Januario.'

The bishop appealed to the doctor to close his clinic and his schools, but that he refused to do. He averred that he was fulfilling a mission that God had entrusted to him, and was being blessed. By divine constraint he must continue his labours with unabated zeal. He was not contravening the Portuguese Constitution by those activities.

The doctor appealed to the supreme judge in Madeira, asking for his ruling on the legality of the arbitrary and hostile treatment to which he was being subjected, and to this appeal various friends of the Kalleys added their voice of protest.

After due consideration the judge issued his ruling, on 31 March 1843: Firstly, there existed no law which condemned the educational and religious teaching exercised by the doctor since he was not infringing any clause of the 1842 Treaty drawn up between Great Britain and Portugal. Secondly, the doctor did not oppose the state religion in public meetings, indeed he did not hold meetings other than in his own residence or that of Protestant sympathizers living in the vicinity, or on occasions, in places like São Jorge, where, with the presence of Catholic clergy, he was invited to expound the Scriptures.

The religious and civil authorities were furious with the judge's findings and took their case to the courts in Lisbon. There, on 5 July 1843, the Madeiran judge's ruling was annulled!

Growth leads to persecution

In 1842 the number of schools increased rapidly. The night schools especially were very popular, all the more so because the Bible was the text-book and explanations of its contents formed part of the lessons. Many of those attending school turned from what they considered to be idolatrous superstitions to a personal, simple faith in Christ as Saviour and Lord. The Bible Society could not supply sufficient Scriptures to meet the demand. Hymns and metric Psalms, prepared by Dr Kalley, were very popular. People sang them as they worked, as they travelled, as they met in school and especially when they were present at Sunday services. These services were held quite openly on the hillside; the hour for conventicles had not yet arrived.

The clergy were increasingly incensed. Opposition became vociferous and abusive under the leadership of a cathedral canon, Carlos de Menezes. His attempts to arouse the ire of people in general at first did not meet with success. From the pulpit he, and others of like mind, inveighed against the 'new sect'. At priests' schools children were taught how to ridicule and mock the 'Calvinists'. Inflammatory pamphlets against these 'readers of the Bible – heretics' were published and widely distributed. Unrelenting effort was made to incite the common people to rise and expel the 'intruder', 'wolf'. Dr Kalley, and to stamp out every vestige of the gospel he proclaimed.

The Free Church of Scotland wrote to Dr Kalley recommending that he leave the island and quoting as a justification Mark 6:11: 'If any place will not receive you and they refuse to hear you, when you leave shake off the dust of your feet as a witness against them.' The doctor replied, 'You quote our Lord's command, "When they persecute you in one city, flee to another." Remember, however, that it is also written in John 10: 12-13, "He who is a hireling and not the shepherd, whose own the sheep are not, sees the wolf coming and leaves the sheep and flees, and the wolf snatches them and scatters them." If I leave them the poor sheep of the flock of Christ will be dealt a terrible blow and the wolf will devour them. The Lord can save me from the fangs of the lion and bear. It is true that he will feed the sheep that are his in my absence; but it is always well to examine ourselves well and truly in order to discern what is the will of God – we must not always fly when we hear the roar of the lion.'

A factor that facilitated the persecution and gave it impetus was the appointing of a new bishop and civil governor, both of whom declared their intention to eradicate the gospel from Madeira and bring about Dr Kalley's expulsion.

Attacks on medical work and schools

In September 1843 the doctor was prohibited from dispensing medicine on the basis of a law which held that only a qualified pharmacist could dispense medicines. He immediately applied to sit the exams necessary to legalize that side of his medical practice, but was informed that if he practised as a pharmacist he could not practise also as a physician: 'Nobody can exercise both professions at the same time!' That was a mortal blow to the doctor's custom of dispensing free medicine for the poor. He confessed: 'What is the use of my treating the poor if I cannot give them medicines and they do not have the means to obtain them?'

The opposition then turned its attention to the schools. The police were ordered to supervise the schools in order to verify that nothing subversive was taught. Dr Kalley was also under constant surveillance, his every move noted. It was impossible for the police to supervise adequately so extensive a network of 'cottage schools' and so the final outcome was that the schools near the capital were forced to close, while those more distant, scattered over the countryside, continued to function.

Believers imprisoned

On 11 January 1843 a teacher, his wife and child, were arrested, accused of civil disobedience and condemned to four months' imprisonment for teaching without an official diploma. On the same day a believer was also condemned to prison for having been caught reading and expounding the Word of God. In April two Madeirans, Nicolau Tolentino and Francisco Pires Soares, converts from Rome, were received into membership by the Scottish Church and partook of the Lord's Supper with the congregation. Both men were well-known and greatly-respected citizens. They were summarily excommunicated by the Roman Catholic Church with all the formalities and publicity: 'Let none give them fire, water, bread, or any other things that may be necessary to them for their support. Let none pay them their debts. Let none support them in any case they may bring judicially. Let all put them aside as rotten, excommunicated members: separated from the bosom and service of the Holy Mother Catholic Church, as rebels and contumacious. For, if any do contrary, which God forbid, I lay, and consider as laid, upon those persons a greater excommunication, etc. and etc.'

These two men were made to suffer to such an extent at the hands of their persecutors that they were forced to hide away in a cave in the mountains for over a year.

It was the conversion, however, of a wealthy, influential man, Arsênio Nicos da Silva, scion of a notable family, which shook the Catholic Church in Madeira to its foundations. Arsênio's only daughter, to whom he was utterly devoted, was taken seriously ill. Local doctors in Funchal were consulted, but all gave the girl up for lost, and in desperation the father appealed to Dr Kalley for help. He visited the patient and confirmed the findings of his Madeiran colleagues that the young girl was indeed gravely ill, but after careful examination and assessment he gave the father a ray of hope. He knelt down and prayed to the Great Healer to guide in the treatment and to bless the girl and her family. The sick girl's condition slowly improved until she was quite recovered. When recovery was assured the father paid a visit to Dr Kalley to express his gratitude and the doctor presented him with a Bible. He read it avidly, keen to understand the meaning of the gospel, and the secret of a consecrated life like that of the doctor. What he read he found disturbing: he could find no biblical basis for the Roman traditions he had been taught to believe. Turning the pages of the New Testament he discovered Peter's epistles – Peter, the first pope! Peter would surely clarify the truth and put doubts to rest, but to his amazement Arsênio found Peter's gospel fully agreed with that of Paul and the other New Testament writers. He heard Dr Kalley preach on the new birth and, shortly afterwards, experienced the new birth for himself. He was now a believer but his wife and daughter, although they loved him, would not follow his spiritual leadership; they remained faithful to the Catholic Church. The priests at first tried to woo Arsênio back to the fold; when that failed they instituted a violent persecution against him. Not only was he himself converted but he was preaching the gospel to others with remarkable results. His total dedication to the gospel cause, and the consequent identification of himself with humble believers, resulted in his losing all his former friends. Persecuted himself, he urged Dr Kalley to continue his ministry and not to abandon the flock. He thought it probable that the day would come when the faithful would have to flee the island, but that day had not yet come!

With the conversion of Arsênio the persecution of believers intensified. Some twenty-six 'heretics' were imprisoned and one, a wealthy farmer, was deported to Portuguese West Africa for the sake of Christ. In prison, mixing with felons and murderers and other assorted criminals, the believers gave good testimony to their steadfast faith in Christ. They derived great comfort from the Word of God and from the singing of the hymns prepared for them by Dr Kalley.

One woman, Maria Joaquina Alves, mother of seven, was

arrested and charged with apostasy, heresy and blasphemy. After sixteen months she was brought to trial to answer the charges made against her. The last charge, blasphemy, was singled out for special attention. 'Do you believe,' she was asked, 'the consecrated host to be the real body and the real blood and the human soul and divinity of Christ?' Her life depended on her answer, but firmly and clearly she replied, 'I do not believe it.' The judge sentenced her to death. About a year later this sentence was nullified by a Lisbon court, but only on the basis of a technical error committed in the trial. The sentence, therefore, could not be carried out. The day after her release she attended a church service and requested to be admitted to membership, as by this time the Madeiran evangelical church had been founded. She became a living example to her fellow-believers of how they were called to suffer for the sake of the gospel and, in suffering, to stand firm for conscience and loyalty to Christ.

The doctor in jail

Dr Kalley's ministry was now severely circumscribed. He could no longer treat the poor, his schools were interdicted and, finally, his preaching was prohibited. As he was later to explain to the General Assembly of the Free Church of Scotland held in Inverness in August 1845, 'About the same time as the law which affected my work as a physician, another directive was given by the tribunal in Lisbon. It was declared to be a criminal act for a British citizen to teach doctrines contrary to the religion of the state, at which persons of Portuguese nationality were present. After I received a copy of the directive, I did not feel free to continue my meetings with the Portuguese brethren and so I ceased to minister to them publicly.'

Church and state conspired against the 'good doctor'. More than once gatherings in his own home were broken up and, finally, on the basis of a law passed by the Inquisition in 1603 against all heresy, the authorities arrested Dr Kalley and imprisoned him. Bail was denied him on the basis that the crime merited the death penalty. In consequence there was a general outcry. The Free Church of Scotland, the London

Missionary Society, together with other British institutions, as well as individuals, combined their efforts to secure Dr Kalley's release. These efforts were not successful. The Portuguese authorities refused to yield to pressure even from such an ally as Britain.

Life in the jail would be spartan, but not impossibly harsh for a man of Dr Kalley's calibre. He would have his own cell, and once a friendly relationship with the jailer had been established – something at which the doctor was especially gifted – the cell door would not be locked and barred. He would certainly be allowed the freedom of the courtyard. As for food, prisoners were expected to feed themselves, or at least pay for the meagre prison fare. The doctor's meals would be cooked in his own home and brought to him by one of the servants. There is no record of his influence on either the jailer or other prisoners, but one thing is certain: they would all have had the gospel explained to them in quiet, friendly conversations. Later, when the persecution became more general and believers were imprisoned for their faith, the jailor would allow one or another to slip out at night to attend a meeting! He knew that he could trust them to return after the meeting! The greatest trial to Dr Kalley was that he had lost his liberty.

Although in jail Dr Kalley received certain privileges, not least among them the right to receive visits. Every Sunday the believers, his spiritual children, queued up outside the prison for a brief visit to him. They were allowed into the prison yard in groups of three, and since the day was not long enough for all to see him they were allowed to come back on weekdays too. Although he was not allowed to read the Bible to them or to sing hymns with them, he had a word of comfort and encouragement for each one. Paul, in his prison in Rome, declared: 'The Word of God is not bound.' Like Paul, Dr Kalley could say, 'My imprisonment is for Christ'. As his friends waited their turn to go into the jail they were subject to all kinds of verbal abuse and even spat on by their enemies who gathered to torment them. The jail was near the cathedral!

Among the visitors that Dr Kalley received while in prison some were very distinguished – the Duchess of Manchester, a fervent practising Christian, an M.P. by the name of Scott, and Captain Allan Gardiner, whose missionary zeal equalled his own. The latter's ship was in port taking on stores. He was on his way to South America – Argentina, Paraguay and Bolivia – to assess the viability of beginning missionary work among the indigenous population, the numerous Indian tribes. Later, what he saw while passing through Brazil convinced him that not only the jungle Indian but also the so-called civilized population stood in dire need of the gospel. There in the prison yard the two men talked freely. Captain Gardiner left on record his impression of the greatness of Dr Kalley and his admiration of the work he had accomplished in so short a period of time. He also lamented that Her Majesty's government should allow a British subject to languish in a foreign jail on trumped-up charges.

In December a unique meeting took place in Dr Kalley's cell. The minute of that meeting is on record in the Scots Church of Funchal of which Dr Kalley was an elder: 'To confirm the nomination of the Rev. Wood for minister of the Free Church of Scotland in this locality. Funchal 15th December 1843. Present: Mr Fullerton, Elder Grant, Dr Kalley, Mr Innes and the Rev. Julius Wood.' The signatories had been sent to Madeira especially to visit Dr Kalley and convey to him the love and concern the church as a whole felt for him.

The queen and the Bibles

In October the Bishop of Madeira, Don Januário Vicente Camacho, issued a pastoral letter to be read in every pulpit. The letter declared that the Bible being distributed on the island, although the Roman Catholic version, translated from the Vulgate by Padre Antônio Pereira de Figueiredo, was falsified; indeed, it was a travesty of the authorized text! Dr Kalley had taken care to request from the Bible Society this Catholic version, without the Apocrypha, rather than the 'Protestant' version of João Ferreira de Almeida, in order that he might reassure Madeirans that the Bible he was giving them was indeed the one authorized by the Catholic Church. The bishop condemned the reading of the Bible and excommunicated, *ipso facto*, anyone either reading or possessing a Bible. Dr Kalley prepared to refute the accusation, but it became unnecessary for him to do so since someone else strenuously defended the authenticity of the Bibles published by the Bible Society. And that person was none other than the Queen of Portugal.

A newspaper of the island of Terceira, in the Azores, while denouncing the accusation made by the bishop, cited an edict promulgated in Lisbon, dated 17 October 1842, which declared as a true version the Bibles the British Consul in Ponta Delegada, Mr Thomas Carew-Hunt, had received from the British and Foreign Bible Society for distribution on Terceira. The article went on to quote that Her Majesty, the Queen of Portugal, with the approval of Archbishop Francisco D. Luiz, had approved the Bible Society version, and had recommended that it be distributed freely on Terceira for the moral and spiritual benefit of her subjects! Dr Kalley needed to add nothing to so valiant a defence.

A temporary respite

With some reluctance the British government did yield to pressure and intervened on behalf of the doctor, through the British ambassador in Lisbon, Lord Howard of Walden. The Court of Appeal of the kingdom of Portugal resolved, on 12 December 1843, that the refusal to grant bail was illegal, as also the arrest and imprisonment of the doctor. The British held that Dr Kalley, as a British citizen resident in Funchal, had in no way contravened articles of the Treaty of 1842. In view of the decision of the Lisbon Court, Dr Kalley was released from prison. He had been confined for six months.

Since his imprisonment had been declared illegal, and no charge was brought against him, he returned to normal activities. He did, however, absent himself from Funchal for a period, he and his wife moving up into a retreat in the mountains, Quinta das Ameixoeiras. This enabled him to concentrate his pastoral gifts on a growing congregation in the mountains at Santo Antônio da Serra. This was to become one of the main centres of evangelical faith on the island. Dr Kalley wrote, 'I was freed from prison in January 1844 and I resumed the work that had been interrupted. I did this because the only judge authorized to give a verdict declared that there had been no breach of law, nor of the country's constitution. The police continued to dog my footsteps, but in spite of every difficulty some six hundred people gathered each Sunday during the summer months for worship in Santo Antônio da Serra, and about thirty on a week-night.' In August that year Dr Kalley celebrated the first communion service in Portuguese, and in September he returned to his home in the Caminho do Monte, in Santa Luzia, Funchal.

The pressures increased. The 'Calvinistic heretics' in general, and Dr Kalley in particular, were accused of creating public disorder. In an effort to defuse the situation and ease the pressure on his flock, Dr Kalley and his wife left Madeira in January the following year and spent a few weeks in Lisbon. He took the opportunity of discussing the situation with the British ambassador in Lisbon and they came to an agreement. Lord de Walden would insist with the Portuguese authorities that all legal proceedings against Dr Kalley should be shelved permanently and the doctor, for his part, would desist in his intention to sue the authorities for unlawful detention in jail.

6.
A church is born

While in Lisbon the Kalleys were surprised to meet the Rev. William Hepburn Hewitson and learn of his mandate. He was on his way to Madeira, having been commissioned by the Free Church of Scotland to care for the Madeiran believers, to organize them into a church with the customary elders and deacons and to extend and develop elementary education. Dr Kalley had not been consulted regarding the appointment of Mr Hewitson, as the doctor was an independent, not having received any help either from the church in Scotland nor yet from the Presbyterian Church in Funchal. A lesser man would have resented such a flagrant lack of courtesy and such deliberate interference. Instead he welcomed his new colleague and together they returned to Madeira.

Soon after their arrival a further crisis arose. Dr Kalley was again apprehended, the charge this time being that he held meetings in his home at which Portuguese citizens were present and taught doctrines contrary to the state religion. This time he was allowed bail. Britain's Foreign Secretary, Lord Aberdeen, had warned Dr Kalley that should he continue to hold meetings at which Portuguese citizens were present his government would not protect him against expulsion from Madeira as an 'undesirable'. The doctor was faced with an insuperable difficulty. If he continued to hold meetings he would be expelled and the Madeirans deprived of his moral and spiritual leadership. He willingly handed over to the Rev. Hewitson, therefore, the pastoral care and administration of the work. He wrote, 'If there were no one to continue my work I would be sorry indeed, but thanks be to God we have here at hand one better than I who can polish these rough diamonds.'

The new pastor

The Rev. Hewitson was a remarkable young man. As a student in Edinburgh he gained the highest academic honours, but in doing so his health, never robust, broke down. Not only was he an intellectual, he was deeply spiritual also. He once wrote, 'The evangelical Christian is one who is so from the heart, the spirit, not the letter; one whose glory is not from men but from God – if Christ be in us then the evidences of his gracious presence are not confused or illegible – the faith that makes for life illuminates as well because faith is precisely the grace of a Saviour who abides in us, and so the Saviour is our life, and that life is the light of men.'

In spite of failing health he implored the church to ordain him and to find a sphere of service for him. Eventually it was thought that Madeira would be a suitable place and he was duly ordained in November 1844 by the Edinburgh Presbytery of the Free Church of Scotland. The Free Church thus assumed jurisdiction over the missionary work in Madeira. The Rev. Hewitson went to Lisbon for three months to learn Portuguese and it was there that he met Dr Kalley. The latter confesses that his young colleague 'began with great zeal and love the work for which God had graciously, and in a manner so extraordinary, prepared him. His presence was providential. May the Lord of the harvest send many such workers into his harvest field.'

The church is established

Quietly and unostentatiously Mr Hewitson gathered together the persecuted flock in a way similar to that in which conventicles were convened and carried through here in Britain in the dark days following the Act of Uniformity in 1662. He celebrated the Lord's Supper for the first time in Portuguese on 25 March 1845. Thirty-four Madeirans sat down at the Lord's Table. Two weeks earlier, in the home of an English lady, Miss Dennison, he had baptized two infants but in the utmost secrecy. The parents had walked four hours during the night in order to arrive at the house under cover of darkness. In spite of the threat of arrest and imprisonment an increasing number of converts applied to the Kirk Session for member-ship and admission to the Lord's Table. The following month sixty-one were received into communion. A witness wrote that what he saw reminded him of gatherings in the early church of New Testament times: 'Many were moved by deep emotion. Mr Hewitson spoke of the prodigal son and I was very impressed by his fluency in Portuguese – his complete command of the language and his excellent pronunciation.' The church was officially organized on 8 May 1845 and elders and deacons duly inducted. It was the first church established on Portuguese soil for Portuguese subjects.

The fact that the Madeiran Church in Funchal was 'pres-byterianized' seemed, to some, to compromise Dr Kalley's position as an independent. He stoutly denied that it was so. 'The organization of a church and the ordination of deacons and elders in Funchal was entirely the work of the Rev Hewit-son, who had been sent by the Free Church of Scotland, with-out my asking. He was in no way under my control. The fact that the Free Church of Scotland is Presbyterian should be sufficient in itself to convince any thinking person that it was not my doing – I am not a Presbyterian nor yet in contact with any kind of church – I am a brother to any Christian irrespec-tive of his denomination' (Dr Kalley to a Mr Reginald S. Smith).

A few days after the establishment of the church Mr Hewit-son wrote to his church in Scotland: 'The horizons are becom-ing increasingly darker. Two or three days ago the Bishop of Madeira stated explicitly at a banquet that he would declare war on the Bible. He went on to say that he had the authorities on his side and that he had resolved to exterminate any who had forsaken the Roman Catholic Church.'

Since the flock was now being well cared for by Mr Hewit-son, Dr Kalley and his wife left in August for a short time of rest and renewal in Scotland.

Mr Hewitson was tireless in his ministry to his scattered congregations. It involved him in continuous and arduous journeys over dangerous mountain paths. The rural Madeirans lived in isolation, the mountainous terrain making it almost impossible to form villages or hamlets. In spite of ill-health, the result of tuberculosis, he visited groups of believ-ers in all parts of the island. The threat of imprisonment was ever present. He received intimation from the chief of police that meetings for Madeirans held in his home must stop or he would be prosecuted. Whimsically he wrote to his church, 'If I am arrested caught taking services I will be sent to prison, but the Lord is my defender. The jailer just now is a good man; he has allowed the believers in jail to slip out at night to attend the meetings. He knows that the believers in the Bible are those who are truly obedient to his Word.'

Threats and persecution did not deter seekers; the number of converts continued to increase. Such was the success of the preaching of the gospel in Madeira that the Rev. Dr Andrew Bonar declared at the Free Church Assembly in May 1846 that it constituted the greatest happening in modern missions. At the end of the year, there were 105 names on the communion roll.

The church under attack

In October 1845 the pace of the persecution accelerated considerably. The believers were subject to increasing harassment by their neighbours, their employers and the authorities. Mr Hewitson described their plight in a report to the Colonial Commission of the Free Church of Scotland: 'People from the Serra are still under arrest and there is no certainty when they will be tried. The number of believers in prison for reading the Word of God is twenty-eight. Six of them were seized a few weeks ago. Their crime was that they had met together on a Sunday evening for mutual edification through reading the Bible and prayer. Three others were arrested at the same time but were afterwards released when the illegality of their arrest was proved. Another family of three were advised that they faced a sentence of seven years deportation to Africa plus a heavy fine. They fled to Demarara before their sentence could be finalized. Those who have embraced the faith, with rare exceptions, are standing firm in spite of the onslaught of persecutors. I am sure that there are many others who read their Bibles secretly and whose only hope of salvation is through faith in Jesus Christ, but they lack the courage to confess him openly. Elijah alone confessed his faith publicly but there were seven thousand who had not bowed the knee to Baal! They worshipped the true God in secret.'

Mr Hewitson's health steadily deteriorated. He had burned himself out. Also the order for his expulsion could not be delayed for long. Indeed, it became inevitable when an evil man, employed by the priests to lead the most violent of the persecutors, was himself converted. Such an act of God's grace was anathema to his employers. Mr Hewitson's fate was sealed – expulsion as an 'undesirable'. Dr Kalley, recently returned from Scotland, strongly advised his colleague to leave Madeira immediately. Reluctantly, therefore, Mr Hewitson embarked for Scotland in May 1846, reassuring his sorrowing parishioners that he would soon be with them again.

7.
The storm bursts

The Supreme Tribunal in Lisbon now ordered that many of the believers detained in prison should be set free. Such clemency served only to incense the persecutors and by August 1846 the storm reached its full fury. The pro-Catholic press advocated the use of violence to curb the threat posed by the 'Calvinistic heretics'. The *Imperial* averred that the only argument that peasants could understand was the lash, the stocks or even hanging. The suggestion was made that there should be another 'St Bartholomew's Night' – the night when, in France, thousands of Huguenots had been massacred. The clergy incited the mob to commit atrocities and believers were cruelly assaulted, beaten with cudgels and in some cases left for dead. Their houses were set on fire and their goods pillaged. The persecutors claimed that there was no law to protect 'Calvinists' and the authorities did not intervene. The perpetrators of violence went unpunished.

Cemeteries were closed to believers. Dr Kalley's first convert, Antônio Fernandes da Gama, died and was refused burial. In vain the British community pleaded that he be allowed to be buried in their private cemetery, but the ecclesiastical authorities would not allow it. They said that he should be made an example and be buried at a cross-roads, so that his grave would be desecrated by the feet of passers-by!

Many in the British colony sympathized with Dr Kalley and greatly admired the work he was doing for the poor. Seventy-seven signed a petition addressed to Lord Howard de Walden in Lisbon: 'We, the under-signed, British subjects, having heard that certain accusations are about to be made by the Governor here to the government in Lisbon, against our much esteemed fellow-countryman, Dr Robert Reid Kalley, and these could affect his continued residence here on the island, we consider such a thing to be a calamity to the inhabitants in general and especially to the poor. We, therefore, wish to inform your Excellency of our esteem for Dr Kalley as a person, and our very real appreciation of his disinterested and untiring benevolence in providing education, both secular and religious, for the poor, as also rendering them free medical care...'

The bishop's accusations

The accusations referred to were carried to Lisbon by the bishop himself. He compiled them into a pamphlet entitled *A Historical Review of the Anti-Catholic Proselytism practised by Dr Robert Reid Kalley, an English doctor, on the Island of Madeira from 1838 until now*. The publication was widely distributed in an endeavour to arouse the sympathy of both religious and secular authorities and pave the way for the violent means about to be employed to silence the doctor and ensure his expulsion from Madeira. The doctor replied by publishing, both in Funchal and Lisbon, his defence, also in pamphlet form, *The Exposition of Facts*, and couched in terms incisive yet courteous.

In his pamphlet the bishop summarized the accusations against Dr Kalley. He was accused of being a Protestant, a Presbyterian, a 'Calvinite' – fanatically so; he was guilty of uninhibited proselytism, and that in a manner both subtle and disarming, under the cloak of philanthropy – free medical treatment for the poor, covering consultation, medicine and, if necessary, hospitalization; free education, with night schools open to all and teachers paid by the doctor or by subscriptions received from British sympathizers. Having brought the unwary and ignorant peasants under his spell, he indoctrinated them with his interpretation of biblical teaching and in doing so attacked the Holy Mother Roman Catholic Church, the state religion. He inveighed against the Trinity, the Virgin Mary, the images of saints, the mass, purgatory and other Catholic dogmas, knowing that the native Madeirans, having been baptized in infancy according to

Catholic ritual were, in their entirety, members of that church; all Madeirans were Catholics. Dr Kalley posed a threat to the whole community of the island: the solidarity and fidelity of the population in general were threatened, and, logically, the state too. He was abusing the goodwill and hospitality Madeira had shown him. Above all, the bishop averred that Dr Kalley, in a personal interview, had promised not to continue his preaching!

Dr Kalley's reply

Dr Kalley, for his part, did two things in his pamphlet: he defended his orthodoxy as a Protestant and took a stand on his civil rights. He dismissed the charges that he did not accept the doctrines of the Trinity and the Virgin Birth. He expounded that all men – Catholic, Protestant or pagan – have come short of the glory of God and need salvation, the salvation which God in mercy provided through the atoning death of his Son, Jesus Christ, a salvation to be received by faith and, that once experienced, leads on to holy living and good works. In preaching the gospel he was obeying the Lord's command: 'Go ye into all the world and preach the gospel.' His preaching was positive. He did not attack the Catholic Church by adopting a negative attitude. He expounded the gospel truths set forth in the Bible, and allowed the truth to speak for itself. Naturally, as a Protestant, he could not accept tradition and dogmas based on tradition. With consummate skill he quoted from the Tridentine rulings as also from a catechism elaborated by Carlos Joaquim Colbert, Bishop of Montpellier (1776).

As to his civil rights, the doctor asked by what law he stood condemned, and quoted the Portuguese constitution, which guaranteed the right of Portuguese citizens to hold their own religious views and prohibited persecution of those who differed from the state religion. He also quoted from the recently updated treaty between Britain and Portugal (1842), which guaranteed the right of a British subject to practise his religion and even, within limits, to build places of worship. The property of a British citizen was held to be inviolate and must be protected by the Portuguese authorities.

He quoted the rulings of two independent Portuguese judges who, on two separate occasions, had thrown out accusations brought against him on the basis that he was holding meetings in his own home at which Portuguese subjects were present. The judges had ruled that there is no law which prohibits a man from receiving visitors in his own home, nor yet legislates on the topics of conversation that take place in the home, religious subjects or otherwise. The doctor rightly held that he had broken no law in showing Christian compassion for the poor – in caring for their physical well-being, in instructing their minds and in meeting their souls' need through Bible teaching.

Mob violence

On 2 August a group of some thirty Madeirans, led by Arsênio, met for prayer and the reading of a letter from the Rev. Hewitson in the home of an English lady, Miss Rutherford, situated in the Quinta das Angustias. She had two sisters living with her at the time, one of whom was gravely ill. As the meeting drew to a close trouble was brewing in the street outside. A mob, led by Canon Telles Menezes, a Jesuit priest, who had been educated in England, gathered outside the house. The few believers who ventured out were made to run the gauntlet; insults and blows were heaped on them. The remainder, mainly women and children, took refuge in the huge kitchen at the back of the house. Miss Rutherford, speaking perfect Portuguese, warned the crowd that what they were doing was against the law, advised them that her sister was very ill and, finally, stated that if they thought that she was harbouring criminals, they could call the police to make the necessary arrests. They demanded that she hand over the Madeirans, which she refused to do.

For hours the crowds milled around the house, shouting obscenities mixed with *vivas* for 'Our Lady of the Mount' and for ' the Holy Mother Roman Catholic Church'. The crowds grew and passions were roused to a fiery pitch which finally erupted in action. The house was stormed, windows were smashed and the door battered down. The crowd rampaged through the ground floor, searching room after room, hoping to flush out any believers who might be lurking in dark recesses. Darkness impeded their progress as there were twenty or more rooms to search! They reached the kitchen at last, and a roar went up; they had discovered the hiding-place.

And the police? The official in charge of the force expected to receive orders from the governor to quell the riot, but no such order came. He acted on his own initiative and he and his men arrived just in time to avoid a massacre. One old man had already been dragged out into the garden, bleeding profusely from a blow on his head; the mob intended to club him to death. The police intervened and soon restored order. They then escorted the believers to their respective homes.

Miss Rutherford protested to the British Consul, as did a certain Captain Tate who had been present in the house at the time of the disorders. Dr Kalley also voiced his protest. The consul would accept no responsibility: 'It is the duty of the police to keep law and order,' he declared. What annoyed him was not that British subjects had suffered harassment by a riotous mob, and their lives had been put in danger, but that Miss Rutherford should have allowed such a meeting to take place in her house! No charge was brought against the leaders of the riot and no enquiry was instituted either by the Portuguese authorities or by the British. Complete anarchy reigned. Crowds vociferated in the streets and thronged the gates of the homes of Miss Rutherford and Dr Kalley. Insults were hurled at anyone entering or leaving their houses; neither life nor property was safe. The authorities did give verbal guarantees, but subsequent events were to prove that they were not to be honoured.

Plot against the doctor

With the removal of the Rev. Hewitson from the island, Canon Telles had directed his fanatical fury against Dr Kalley. Rumours indicated that a definite plot was hatched to kill Dr Kalley and ransack his house and hospital in Santa Luzia, and these were continued. The consul was warned that the doctor was in danger of his life, but the warning went unheeded. The doctor then appealed to the chief of police, but his messenger was severely mauled by the mob. The civil governor, the highest authority in Madeira, when appealed to, showed only hostility. He accused the doctor of being the cause of all the disturbance, and said that it was 'the fruit of the tree which the doctor had planted, a tree capable of producing only discord and confusion'. The governor reiterated his determination to eradicate Protestantism from the island, at least from among the Madeirans. When he took office in 1843 he had declared that he would use all his powers to root out Bibles and Bible readers from the territory under his jurisdiction. It was common talk that Dr Kalley would not escape this time, 'unless he is the devil in person'.

During the week events moved rapidly. English families known to sympathize with the gospel cause were subject to constant harassment by lawless gangs. Behind it all moved Canon Telles and other clerics stirring up hatred and violence. Mrs Kalley and other ladies found refuge in the British consulate. The consul had deliberately chosen to absent himself and spend time in his country residence in the hills! By Saturday, the 8th, it was patent to Dr Kalley that he could not rely on any form of protection, whether Portuguese or British. With the aid of friends he sought to barricade windows and doors. The chief of police had sent a posse of police to guard the gate to the courtyard and house, but the doctor overheard them discussing with a group of masked men whether the attack should begin there and then or whether they should await the pre-planned signal! By two o'clock in the morning bolts and bars were secured and the doctor disguised himself as a peasant. His friends insisted that he must escape at once. He did so by climbing over a back wall into a vineyard and so up the hill to a safe house. His friends followed him over the wall and dispersed.

Madeira's 'St Bartholomew's Day'

Sunday, 9 August, dawned, and this year, according to expectation, Madeira's 'St. Bartholomew's Day'. Canon Telles harangued a densely-packed congregation in the cathedral: 'Defend your patron saint, Our Lady of the Mount; defend the Holy Mother Roman Catholic Church; pacific methods of preventing the spread of heresy have

failed, violent methods are now called for; show your zeal for
the religion of your forefathers by violently ejecting "Calvinists" and laying waste their properties; your weapons are
now sword and fire.'

Outside the cathedral, in the square, a rocket swished into
the air, quickly followed by a second. The signal had been
given and its repercussions were felt all over the land. 'St
Bartholomew's Day' had begun. Violence erupted in the city
and eventually spread throughout the island. The 'Calvinist
heresy' was to be uprooted once and for all.

The houses and small-holdings of believers came under systematic attack. A British naval officer, who sympathized with
the persecuted, recorded: 'Every day we hear of new cases of
violence and cruelty against believers. They are left with no
other alternative than to flee for their lives.' Hebrews 11: 36-
38 was being re-enacted. In Santo Antônio da Serra and in
Lombo das Faias the authorities forced an entry into the
houses of believers during the night and put to flight the
families who lived there. The police and soldiers regaled
themselves freely on anything they found – wine, pigs, hens,
stored grain; anything and everything was pillaged. It was a
'scorched earth' policy. The believers were left homeless and
destitute. Women and girls were subjected to indignities and
the men cruelly beaten. Twenty-eight men and women, some
of them girls, were crowded into a foul dungeon, but from the
dungeon a song was heard, one of Dr Kalley's hymns: 'Here
we suffer grief and pain ...' It was an eloquent testimony to
the indomitable spirit of the sufferers.

Those were days of agony for anyone associated with the
evangelical movement, even those of British nationality. The
Madeirans who could escape went into hiding in the woods
and caves of the mountains, but even there they were not
safe. Their enemies pursued them relentlessly. The civil
authorities had completely lost control. Roving bands of
marauders went on the rampage, some criminal but others
motivated by the thought that they were on a sacred crusade
against heretics. Naturally, the more moderate among the
population and foreigners resident in Funchal were horrified
at what was taking place and protested vigorously against
such fanaticism and barbarity.

And what of Dr Kalley on that fateful day? The crowd, led

by Canon Telles, surged out into the narrow streets and on towards Santa Luzia. They chanted orchestrated slogans as they went: 'Long live Our Lady of the Mount!' 'Long live the Holy Mother Roman Catholic Church', 'Death to the Wolf from Scotland,' 'Death to Kalley'. The full tide of enmity and hatred was concentrated on the doctor.

The crowd positioned themselves in the street and at a given signal stormed the house and hospital. Barricades were swept aside and the howling mob of thugs, vowing vengeance, searched the house. It was empty. Dr Kalley was not there and it was he the crowd wanted; they were intent on dragging him out into the street and lynching him. The governor of the island and the chief of police were present, apparently intent on seeing that the work of destruction was carried through thoroughly! The British consul rode up on horseback, too late to be of the least service. Not finding the doctor, the crowd vented their spite on his belongings. Household and hospital furnishings, together with a valuable collection of books, were taken out into the street and burned and no effort was made to quell the riot.

Escape

The search for the doctor continued relentlessly. He had found refuge in the house of two brothers, his converts, in the Quinta da Boa Vista. His life was in danger and a way had to be found to get him on board the safety of a British vessel anchored in the harbour and ready to sail for the West Indies. The consul was of the opinion that he should be escorted through the town to the landing-place on the beach by the governor and a company of soldiers. When she heard of it Mrs Kalley opposed the idea. Rightly, she believed that in such company her husband would be in still greater danger – the governor was his declared enemy, the soldiers were treacherous and the mob thirsting for his blood. Neither his wife nor his friends would countenance such a plan, so they devised an ingenious, but still extremely dangerous method of escape. In Funchal there were various forms of transport: a sledge pulled over the cobbled streets by oxen, a litter carried by porters, and the hammock, slung on a pole and carried by relays of porters – a method usually employed for carrying a sick person from one place to another. A hammock was obtained and with extreme difficulty porters were hired. Dr Kalley was then disguised as an old sick woman! When he was in the hammock complete disguise was made possible by the custom of covering the sick person from head to foot with a sheet. The bearers were suspicious. They suspected that they were carrying a bogus patient, and a heavy one at that! More than once they put the hammock down and declared they would go no further. All the time, on their way into town, they were passing knots of people discussing the events of the day. The mob was now certain that the doctor had managed to reach the British consulate, so they conglomerated there, demanding that the doctor should be handed over to them. One of the bearers gave up when they were within sight of the crowd, and the situation became desperate. Another porter was pressed into service and the journey towards the beach resumed. During the delay someone noticed that Dr Kalley's servant was helping with the hammock. The cry went up: 'Kalley! Kalley!' The cry re-echoed from street to street but, in the confusion that arose, the bearers were able to reach the shore before the mob set off in hot pursuit. The ship's boat was waiting and the hammock was bundled into it. Minutes afterwards, a frustrated rabble, milling around on the beach, watched the boat pull away towards the ship.

Meanwhile, those still outside the consulate were working themselves into a frenzy. Their insistent demand was that Dr Kalley should be brought out of hiding. They invaded the courtyard and raised the cry: 'Fire! Bring fire!' The perilous situation was finally brought under control by the ship's captain who had arrived to enquire of the consul regarding Dr Kalley. With courage and determination he faced the crowd, persuaded them that the doctor was not in the consulate but on board his ship, the *Forth*. He expelled them from the premises, dispersed them and restored order. Later, Mrs Kalley joined her husband on board. They were safe, but they had lost everything: personal belongings, property, furnishings, books – all had been consigned to the flames.

Fires continued to burn. On the hillsides cottages, which had once housed his schools, the homes of his beloved flock,were ablaze and bonfires of Scriptures were alight in the central square. The rioting mob had run amok, ransacking, looting and burning. In the evening the *Forth* weighed anchor and set sail for the West Indies, but back in Madeira the bishop issued a pastoral letter, to be read to the 'faithful' from the pulpit at mass in every parish church. It read: 'The Lord, having compassion on your troubled situation, condescended to incite and direct by way of moderation and charity, your purified religious zeal and national energy, and by an extraordinary mode, and perhaps strange in the eyes of the world, to snatch from the midst of you, his flock, already torn to pieces, that wolf from Scotland.'

The following paragraph is part of a sermon by Dr Kalley rescued from the fire in Madeira, based on Isaiah 53:10: 'The pleasure of the Lord shall prosper in his hand.'

'The prosperity of religion is the great object of the true Christian. He longs for this, he prays for this and for this he labours – for this he lives and for this he could die. The salvation of souls is the delight of God. It is in the hands of Christ. It must prosper in his hands... Some men have their chief enjoyment in eating and drinking...Some in adding field to field and there have been men of blood whose dark souls found their pleasures in the battlefield and, it seems in trampling under foot their fellow men. The delight of God – his pleasure – is conformable to his character, to the grand distinguishing attribute of his being. In every man's character there is generally some marked feature, some distinguishing characteristic. One has a vivid imagination, another a clear sound head, and others have remarkable energy, decision of character... That of God is love. And what could afford more pleasure, more delight to a being of such character than the salvation of souls? What could gratify – or (may I use the word) indulge – his loving goodness more than delivering from hell...?'

8.
Out of the ashes . . .

What of the sheep now without their shepherd?

Having completed the devastation in Funchal the persecutors concentrated their fury and violence on the scattered sheep who had taken refuge in the dense woods and mountain fastnesses. These fanatical persecutors have been described as ferocious, hungry wild animals and they certainly behaved as such. There in the mountains believers were, to a certain extent, shielded by those among them who knew the secrets of safe hide-outs, and these also, at great risk to themselves, supplied them with food whenever possible. During the first two weeks after Dr Kalley's escape the remorseless 'holy crusade' continued unabated. Arrests were daily occurrences and no mercy was shown to those found guilty of being Bible readers. There was no justice either. Crippling fines were imposed, and even those imprisoned were forced to pay for the expense of their imprisonment! All were excommunicated and the curse of the church pronounced over them. That meant that no one would sell them food, or do business with them. They were ostracized and treated as pariahs. Miraculously there was only one martyr, Antônio Martins; he was cruelly beaten to death.

The believers flee

There was only one option open to these souls in tribulation for the sake of Jesus Christ, and that was to flee the island. By coincidence, at the time of these demonstrations of bigotry and intolerance in Madeira, the British were recruiting labourers to work the sugar plantations in the West Indies. The slaves had been freed and manpower was at a premium. Madeira was one of the ports of call made by vessels specially chartered to convey workers to the Caribbean. As the initial fury of persecution began to die down, at the end of August, the *William* of Glasgow anchored in the bay. Arrangements were made for the ship's boats to pick up refugees secretly by night from quiet inlets along the shore and convey them to the vessel. They escaped with their lives, but all their possessions were left behind and lost. So ill-clad were the refugees that the crew gave them clothing. Amongst these Madeirans were some who, like Saul of Tarsus, had thought that they were doing God service by persecuting Bible readers but, through the quiet, steadfast witness of the persecuted, they had been won over to the faith, and now they in turn suffered persecution!

When the *William* sailed for the West Indies on 23 August more than 200 believers were crowded on board. To leave their native land so suddenly and unexpectedly was to them heart-rending, but they were together, united in suffering by the bonds of love in Christ, and filled with hope that in the New World to which they journeyed they would be free to worship God according to the dictates of their conscience. A few days later a further 500 of their brethren followed them aboard the *Lord Seaton*. In the months that followed the authorities supplied the Protestant emigrants of conscience with exit visas – it was an excellent way of ridding the island of the obnoxious 'Calvinists'. A total of over 2000 left Madeira for Trinidad, Antigua, St Kitts, Demerara and Jamaica.

The British government eventually obliged the Portuguese authorities in Lisbon to pay Dr Kalley damages for the heavy losses he had sustained, but the rank and file of the Madeirans received no compensation whatever for the material losses they had sustained. For them it was a completely new start in life, but now with Christ. Dr Kalley invested the compensation he received, using the proceeds to help Madeirans and, later, Brazilians in the task of evangelization.

On 30 October 1846, the bishop, in an article in the local newspaper, trounced the 'Wolf from Scotland' and exhorted the faithful: 'Let us join our prayers to those of the Holy

Church in thanksgiving to the Lord for having delivered his people from the pestilence of heresy with which, in the days of his wrath, he visited them.' Church and state thought that they had eradicated completely from the island the Bible and its readers. How deceived they were!

Arrival in the West Indies

In Acts chapter 8 we read: '... a great persecution arose against the church ... and they were all scattered ... those who were scattered went about preaching the word'. As in Palestine, so in Madeira. Persecution scattered the believers but did not dim their testimony. The Madeirans arrived in the West Indies in levies; group after group disembarked in Trinidad and on the neighbouring islands. Work was not difficult to find since, slavery having been abolished, the sugar plantations absorbed their labours easily. The torrid climate, however, so different from that of their native land, proved to be debilitating, even unbearable. Many were taken ill and a few died. The situation became so serious that the Governor of Trinidad, Lord Harris, intervened and had the Madeirans moved to plantations of coffee and cocoa high in the hills where the temperature was cooler and which were more shaded from the fierce rays of the sun. The immigrants had difficulty with the language too, but they were able to communicate their gratitude for all the kindnesses they received from the English-speaking inhabitants of the islands. The Portuguese have a natural bent for commerce and soon a few of the newly arrived Madeirans managed to establish themselves in small businesses and in different crafts – as barbers, cobblers, tailors, carpenters, etc.

As believers they had been well schooled in biblical living by Dr Kalley and the Rev. Hewitson and maintained their testimony. They were Puritans by spiritual upbringing and continued to live simple, pious lives in their new surroundings. In this they differed from Caribbean churchgoers, brought up in a more liberal and less demanding tradition. Ethnically the Madeirans differed from the inhabitants too, and that contributed also to their isolation. They maintained their own services, meeting as they had done in Madeira for normal

Sunday services, Bible Study and prayer meetings. In Port of Spain as many as 300 would gather on Sunday and their fervour, their biblical testimony, influenced many from outside their circle, resulting in constant conversions.

Visit of Mr Hewitson

In January 1847 the Rev. Hewitson was commissioned by the Colonial Council of the Free Church of Scotland to visit Trinidad: 'not only to bring comfort to the flock but also to reorganize the church in an orderly manner, adapted to its new environment'. *En route*, the Rev. Hewitson paid a quiet, unostentatious visit to Madeira to strengthen the believers and to encourage new converts. The church in Madeira had been decimated but had survived the persecution and was growing. In Trinidad the Rev. Hewitson received a joyous welcome. He wrote describing the scene: 'The meeting was for both pastor and flock a joyous occasion. The ties of affection that had bound us together as one, from Madeira onwards, ties that had been strengthened by perils and difficulties, were more than enough to ensure that the manifestations of mutual joy were far above the ordinary.' He organized schools for Madeiran children during the day and for adults at night. He also prepared new converts for baptism and church membership, making sure that they had not only the Word of God but also the anointing of the Spirit. In spite of delicate health the missionary-cum-pastor journeyed incessantly, his itinerary covering the island of Trinidad, as also other islands where there were members of his old flock.

His letters of that period show how indefatigable he was: 'Yesterday I went to Santa Cruz, some ten miles from here, seeking out Madeiran believers. I found twenty living on the same farm and we held a service after they had finished the labours of the day. It was an excellent meeting. This climate does not help my sickness!' 'Last Wednesday I left here in a conveyance a little after six in the morning and journeyed ten miles. I preached to forty Madeirans in the open under the shade of a tree. I afterwards went about six miles and preached to another twenty Portuguese, this time in a shed. I returned a few miles and again preached in a small town to a group of believers who had come together for a meeting, from a radius of two miles or so, after the day's labour. After breakfast, on Thursday, I left the village. If God wills I hope to go there again on Sunday to administer the Lord's Supper and preach twice. Last Sunday I gave communion to about eighty Portuguese.'

In May the Rev. Hewitson took a tearful farewell of his beloved flock and embarked for Glasgow. In the short space of three months he had reorganized the church and laid the foundations for a spiritually prosperous future, as well as founding schools for children and adults. On arrival in Scotland he served as minister in Dirleton for a short period but he still kept in touch with his brethren overseas. He died on 7 August 1850, victim of the insidious disease that had dogged his footsteps since his student days, tuberculosis.

Arsênio as pastor

During the latter part of his ministry in Trinidad, the Rev. Hewitson had been greatly helped and encouraged by Arsênio. After the debacle of 9 August, Arsênio had been forced to flee with others to the hills. He owned properties there, and for a time was able to subsist. He did not accompany the groups that sought refuge in the Caribbean, since he was most desirous of beginning a new life with his wife and daughter, if possible, in mainland Portugal. He endeavoured to visit his home secretly at night, but discovered that the house was under continual surveillance; his persecutors anticipated such an attempt and were ready to arrest him. Not being able to talk to his wife, he got into touch with her through a trusted servant, expounded his plan to set up home in Portugal and asked her for money for the journey. She sent the money but gave no hope of following him to the mainland. He sought refuge in Oporto and it was there that a letter from Dr Kalley reached him. The doctor suggested that he proceed to Trinidad and there take over the pastorate of the flock. He accepted the challenge and travelled to the Caribbean. The Free Church of Scotland ordained him to serve the brethren in Port of Spain and there, for two years, he laboured assiduously.

Towards the end of 1847 the situation of the refugees from Madeira worsened considerably. The West Indies and the sugar industry were in serious financial straits. The Madeirans had arrived stripped of all they possessed, and they were unable to earn enough to maintain even their simple life-style. The Free Church of Scotland, doubtless as a result of the Rev. Hewitson's report, entered into negotiations with the American Protestant Society and the American Christian Union requesting '... the grant of land, good for cultivation in the United States, where they [the Madeirans] can live near one another, build a church and start a school for their children, and where they can honestly earn their daily bread and render to the Lord God worship in spirit and truth'. In reply, assurance was given that the Madeiran brethren would be given a warm welcome, land to cultivate and financial aid.

The Rev. Arsênio was taken ill, so gravely that the church insisted that he accompany an emissary of the American Protestant Society back to New York to receive specialized treatment. He had hopes of continuing his journey as far as the 'promised land' in the state of Illinois, but his condition worsened. As he lay dying he made one last request, that a letter be sent to his wife, telling her of his death, and exhorting her to read again his letters to her and to meditate on the gospel truths contained therein. Arsênio had sacrificed his all – family, fortune, country, health – and had died among strangers in a foreign land. He had indeed 'counted all things but loss for the excellency of the knowledge of Christ', for whom he could say, 'I suffered the loss of all things and count them but dung, that I may win Christ.' Win Christ he did, and even the strangers among whom he found himself at the end were awed by his Christ-like life and utter dedication. His flock followed north to the United States, and successive groups of believers were soon on their way to either New York or Baltimore. And so began the most extraordinary accretion to the Protestant population in the U.S.A.

Illinois

One Sunday in November 1848 a group of over 100

Madeirans disembarked in Baltimore. They were enthusiastically received, given warm winter clothing and lodging. The
Presbyter Francisco de Souza Jardim wrote, 'Only by the
divine intervention of our good God, after all the persecution
we have suffered in the cause of the gospel, and that in our
own land, can we now be received with open arms in a strange
land and all our needs supplied.'

The American Protestant Society went the 'second mile' by
sending out an envoy, the Rev. Manoel G. Goncalves, to
Trinidad. He himself was a Madeiran but while he was still a
child his parents had emigrated to the States. There he was
converted, studied and was ordained a minister by the Baptist
Church for a specific service, to evangelize several hundred
Portuguese from the Azores, who were working as fishermen
on the New England coast. No one was equipped better than
he to assess the situation of the believers, his own fellow-
countrymen, in the West Indies. He was amazed at the sincerity and simplicity of their faith and even more at the privations
they had endured for the sake of the gospel. He wrote, 'These
people have sacrificed property, goods, family and friends,
and country too – everything for the gospel and obedience to
God's behests.'

On returning to the States he raised funds and support for
the final phase of the evacuation of believers from the West
Indies to the States. Three ships were chartered and in May
1849 no less than 500 embarked, anxious to start life afresh in
North America. Land was granted to the colony of exiles
between Jacksonville and Springfield in Illinois. Some 300
who made the trip from New York by sea and the Great Lakes
were well received by the churches in both towns and given
every help to see them established on their new property. The
language barrier still constituted a difficulty, as also the
brusque change from a torrid climate in the Antilhas to the
temperate zone of the northern States.

A second and third group followed and eventually a considerable colony was well established and thriving in Illinois.
God had also prepared spiritual leaders for the churches. At
the height of the persecution in Madeira two young and promising converts had been sent to Scotland to study in the Divinity Hall of Glasgow University. The Portuguese churches,
Presbyterian in their form of government, in the Jacksonville-

Springfield area, requested the Free Church of Scotland to ordain these young men and send them out to take charge of the flock. The Rev. Antônio de Matos was duly ordained and despatched immediately to the States and inducted into the pastorate. The other young man, the Rev. Henrique Viera, was sent to Trinidad to take charge of the thriving congregation there.

Back in Madeira a few Bibles escaped the bonfires. They were carefully hidden in safe places – even under the hearthstones of cottages. At night these Bibles were taken out and studied by small groups which met for that purpose. The flame of the true faith flickered at first but, fanned by the unabated fury of religious zealots, far from being quenched it burned ever brighter. The authorities on the island were nonplussed at the continuous stream of Madeirans opting for freedom of worship even though it meant exile in a strange land. Many sought refuge in North America, having heard of the wonderful freedom their fellow-believers enjoyed there. They received financial help for the journey from Dr Kalley and friends in Scotland. The colony in Illinois eventually grew to well over a thousand. A good number remained in Madeira and were the means of revitalizing the Scottish Church in Funchal, as well as establishing churches of their own in chosen centres on the island.

Dr Kalley's staunch adherence to his high calling in Christ Jesus and his steadfast endurance in the face of bitter persecution received an abundant reward: a thriving church in Trinidad, an even more prosperous Christian community in Illinois and, miraculously, out of the ashes rose a strong church in Madeira. The blood of the martyrs is indeed the seed of the church.*

*An indication of the impact made by Dr Kalley on Madeira is that no history of nineteenth-century Madeira is complete without some reference to him and his evangelical crusade.

Interlude

interlude

9.
A pause and a person

During all these persecutions and changes for the Madeiran believers, what had happened to the Kalleys?

On their return from that enforced journey to the West Indies in January 1847 they had settled in St Leonards-on-Sea, Sussex, but not for long. The Master's command and the plight of the poor and needy urged the doctor on. He began a period of peripatetic ministry, first in Ireland, then in Malta and, finally, in Palestine. True to his calling as a medical missionary and as a man of independent means, he was free to roam abroad in the gospel cause.

Ireland

The Potato Famine in Ireland had begun in 1842 and had devastated the country. Five years later, in the aftermath of the disaster, poverty, hunger, disease and utter misery still prevailed among the decimated population. Such flagrant need there so challenged the doctor that he moved from the comfort and ease of the Sussex coast to Cork, the centre of a distressed area. As always, he immediately dedicated himself and his calling to the service of those in clamant need of his help. Delving into his own resources he provided not only the medicines he prescribed but food also. He found Irish Roman Catholicism just as fanatical as Madeiran, but he studiously avoided any confrontation. He had come to Ireland not to attack Catholic beliefs but to heal the sick and care for the needy and, in his own unobtrusive way, to make known to them the comforts of the gospel. The damp atmosphere of

Southern Ireland, though, proved detrimental to Mrs
Kalley's health and since her well-being was a constant preoc-
cupation to her husband, after three months they moved to
Malta's more amenable climate.

Death of Mrs Kalley

While in Malta the doctor worked as a medical missionary, an
educationalist and an evangelist. The climate was still not
suitable for Mrs Kalley so two years later, having left his mark
on Malta, they moved to Beirut, hoping that the renowned
healthy climate of the Lebanon would prove beneficial to her.
They made their home in the hills beyond the city and he
devoted himself to nursing his wife, whose condition was
rapidly deteriorating. For years she had had the desire for
believer's baptism, convinced that her christening as a child
was not baptism in the New Testament sense. She intended to
be baptized as a public act of witness but owing to ill-health
had to be content with a private ceremony. On Tuesday, 7
January 1851, in a simple but moving ceremony in the home
the doctor baptized his wife by sprinkling. A few months
later, on 15 September, she died and was buried in Beirut.
The burial service was conducted both in English and Arabic
at the doctor's insistence, as he wanted Arab mourners to
hear of the Christian hope, the resurrection. Mrs Kalley had
been a shadow in the background of her husband's missionary
activity, her health apparently never allowing her to take an
active part in it. Any mention of her is incidental and in passing. To the end, right through the years of their married life
her husband had shielded, cared for and cherished her and
she, loyal to him, suffered with him for the sake of the gospel.
Limited by ill-health and 'in journeyings oft', she had borne
the heat and burden of the day.

Dr Kalley had printed on the reverse side of the card
intimating his wife's death: 'Dear fellow mortal, have you
heard the cry: "Behold, I come quickly, as a thief in the
night"? It is the voice of the Son of God. Are you ready? Have
you felt that as a sinner you are ruined for eternity? Is your
only hope in Jesus – Jehovah, our Righteousness? Are you

rejoicing in him? Are you serving him with a glad heart under the guidance of his Spirit in that work at which you would like to be found at his coming? If so, onward in his name – Watch! Dr Kalley, Beirut, 15 Sept. 1851.'

Palestine

After his wife's death the doctor was free to do something that he had long desired to do and that was explore Palestine. Ever since his conversion and his initial study of prophecy and its fulfilment, he had longed to see for himself the land of God's choice for his people, the Jews.

In the Holy Land he travelled extensively and became an authority on its history, geography and customs. Part of the time he accompanied a fellow Scot and missionary, Dr William M. Thomson, author of *The Land and the Book*. One place where he spent some time was Safed, possibly the 'town set on a hill' to which our Lord referred in the Sermon on the Mount, since it was built into the hillside, the houses rising tier on tier, the roofs of one row serving as the 'street' for the next higher up. It had been completely devastated by an earthquake and when Dr Kalley settled there for a period it was rising again out of the heaps of rubble. It was a town with a history. The Crusaders built a castle there and held it as one of their strong points. To the Jews it was one of the four 'holy towns' in Israel where the precepts of the law were fanatically obeyed and where prayers were offered weekly to 'save the world from destruction'. In fact, according to rabbinical lore it will one day be the seat of the throne of the Messiah. Appropriately, since it was near the tombs of great rabbinical scholars, Hillel among them, a famous rabbinical school was located there. In spite of its status as 'holy', life in the Jewish section of the town was 'a mere loathsome misery, for the people are intolerably dirty and their quarters so foul that fever breaks out when the rain stirs the mud in their lanes'. It was probably the struggle of a community to rebuild their lives in conditions of such abject poverty and misery after the earthquake disaster that attracted Dr Kalley to Safed. It constituted a challenge to the doctor, being a testing ground for his medical skill and missionary zeal. By the time he left he had organized a small congregation composed of Moslems, Jews and Nestorian Christians.

Two lives – one stream

It was Beirut, however, that became a turning-point in Dr Kalley's life; it marked the end of one phase and the beginning of another. In March 1852 he was due to leave Beirut for Scotland but discovered that the ship would sail on Sunday. It was against his principles to begin a journey like that on the Sabbath, so he delayed sailing. While he waited he was asked by a Mr Wilson to see his son, who was dangerously ill with tuberculosis. The young man had been sent to Egypt in an attempt to effect a cure for his malady, but he was now with his father and eldest sister, Sarah Poulton Wilson, in Beirut. Dr Kalley could do nothing for the young man and he died shortly afterwards. But as a result the doctor was to become friendly with the Wilson family, and especially with Sarah. She had heard of the persecution in Madeira and was more than interested to meet the medical missionary involved. Dr Kalley returned to England by ship with the Wilsons, and during the voyage he and Sarah were often in each other's company engrossed in conversation. Their friendship grew into love and in December 1852 they were married in Albany Road Congregational Church, Torquay.

Life took on a new dimension. His whole life and ministry were enriched. It could hardly have been otherwise, since Mrs Sarah Kalley was a talented and irresistibly attractive personality. She exercised a moulding influence on all who came to know her. Sarah Poulton Kalley and Robert Reid Kalley complemented each other. There are some couples whose lives are so intertwined that it is impossible to separate them as, for example, Priscilla and Aquila in Scripture. One is never mentioned without the other. After their marriage it was the same with Sarah and Robert: they were inseparable. His biography becomes their biography.

Sarah was born in Nottingham in 1825. Her father, William Wilson, was a wealthy industrialist and her mother, also Sarah, was a sister of the famed politician of the Victorian

*Dr Robert Reid Kalley and his wife
Sarah Poulton Kalley*

era, Samuel Morley. Her mother died while she was still young and her early years were spent partly in her own home and partly with her mother's relatives, the Morleys, in London. From her earliest years she showed a genuine enthusiasm for life: it brimmed over in vitality and lively humour. With maturing years this characteristic remained undimmed. She retained her youthful zest for life and even in old age still attracted young people to herself. She was very intelligent and, belonging to a wealthy family, was well-educated, speaking both French and German fluently, having travelled extensively on the continent. Her artistic gifts were many: music, poetry, painting – she was talented in them all. Some of her water-colours still exist and amply demonstrate her skill as an artist. Her talents in music and poetry were to be put to good use in later years.

Her greatest asset, however, was her deep, abiding spirituality. Early in life she dedicated herself to Christ and his service, whole-heartedly and with a singleness of purpose. For her to live was Christ. Her initial opportunity for Christian service came in Torquay. A calamity in the family, tuberculosis, brought the whole family to that seaside resort in Devon, said to be an ideal place for the treatment of the so-called 'white plague'. Sarah herself was not affected but two of her brothers were and both died in spite of intensive care and treatment at home and abroad.

In Torquay Sarah joined the Albany Road Congregational Church, built by her father, and at that time a centre for non-conformist activity in the town. The church ran a school not only for poor, deprived children, but also for adults. In the school Sarah had a Bible class for young teenage boys. She exercised a powerful, moulding influence on these youngsters, many of whom became committed Christians and dedicated workers for Christ both in the homeland and overseas. An intimate friend declared that as she matured in life and experience 'saintliness shone in her face'. When she gave an address, whether in the informality of the drawing room, or on more formal occasions in church, she did so in a manner 'lively and sparkling with humour and yet of a deep reverence as she spoke of our Lord and of his saving work'.

Her minister in Albany Road, the Rev. Nicholas Hurry, wrote, 'I made her acquaintance in 1848 when I became pastor of Albany Road, Torquay, and found how earnest and intelligent and successful a teacher she was. She was then beginning a course of usefulness which, thank God, she was honoured to continue until now.' Her faith in the Saviour, her earnest love for him and her concern for the redemption of sinners were paramount in her life.

'Behind every great man there is a woman.' That saying is particularly applicable to Dr Kalley.

A new beginning

During the two years immediately following their marriage, the doctor and his wife paid what was to prove his final visit to the Madeirans in the West Indies and North America. In both places they received a rapturous welcome. In Trinidad, where most of the believers in the Caribbean now lived, the doctor conducted services, Bible Studies and, with his wife, visited individual believers in their own homes. Brotherly love was much in evidence. Dr Kalley and his flock had suffered together in Madeira and the bonds of mutual love and esteem bound them closely together.

In Illinois the welcome was equally cordial. The Madeirans declared a day's holiday to celebrate the arrival in their midst of their beloved pastor. It was a day of high festival – a thanksgiving service with hymn-singing, feasting and, also, tears of joy. Dr Kalley engaged in intensive pastoral and evangelistic activity while Mrs Kalley taught piano to youngsters and held regular singing practices for the congregation as a whole. She rightly believed that the true church is a singing church, and that congregational singing should be of the highest quality. As a result of these months of dedicated labour the church grew considerably.

While there, seeing personally the blessings enjoyed by these Madeirans, formerly persecuted but now happily settled in their promised land, the doctor intensified his efforts to attract to Illinois more of the flock still suffering in Madeira. Many emigrated, the expenses of the journey being met by the doctor and American friends. Dr Kalley insisted that it was the bounden duty of these Portuguese-speaking Madeirans to make Christ known in any part of the world where Portuguese was spoken. He himself set the example, for it was while he was in Springfield, Illinois, that he seriously considered the possibility of another sphere of service. At his age, nearing fifty, lesser men would have been content to retire, but the doctor's dynamic nature would not allow him to rest. In a letter to Springfield, written from Nottingham in January 1855, he made a request: 'Please pray that God may open a way to the sphere of service in which he would have me engage. I sincerely hope that it will be among the Portuguese-speaking peoples where there is, as yet, no Bible nor preachers of the gospel; and if this so happen perhaps some of you may feel great joy in prayer and service in order that the truth of God may be made known among those who speak your language. However, nothing certain is contemplated for the time being.'

While in the States Dr Kalley read the Rev. Daniel Kidder's book *Sketches of Residence and Travels in Brazil.* Kidder, a missionary of the American Methodist Church, recounted so vividly his experiences as a colporteur in Brazil from 1837 to 1842, that the perusal of the book made a lasting impression on the doctor's mind. He began to wonder whether Brazil could be his next sphere of service.

Kidder was a cultured man and prudent in his approach to the problem of introducing the gospel into Brazil. His attractive personality made him very acceptable to the Brazilians and a welcome guest in their homes. He made many friends among the wealthy and influential and introduced them to the Bible. With their help he attempted to induce the authorities to introduce the Bible as a text-book in state schools! The clergy intervened decisively and the attempt was frustrated. A Church of England clergyman, in conversation with a Roman Catholic bishop, heard to his amazement that the version which Kidder wished to introduce into the schools was a truncated version, full of errors! It was the Figuereido version, with the imprimatur of the Roman Church – a crass ignorance on the part of the bishop which Dr Kalley would appreciate! Kidder travelled widely, principally in the state of São Paulo, and at least on one occasion left a stock of Scriptures with a parish priest who had offered to distribute them among his parishioners!

Kidder returned to the States leaving no tangible results of his stay in Brazil: no converts, as far as is known, and certainly no church established. Where so able a man as Kidder had failed could anyone else succeed? That question was uppermost in the doctor's mind during the next few months as he and his wife pondered the possibilities. They were both greatly moved by the spiritual destitution of the Brazilians, and felt that Dr Kalley's previous experiences in Madeira had been a sound preparation for service in Brazil. His familiarity with Portuguese culture, his fluency in the language and, above all, his knowledge of the ways of Rome, qualified him for the work of propagating the gospel in Brazil.

Just at that time a letter was received from the Rev. R. Baird of the American Bible Society requesting that two or three of the Illinois believers be employed as colporteurs in Brazil. The suggestion had originally come from Kidder, but it was one with which the doctor could not agree. He knew that the Bible Society, of necessity, must publicize the activities of its agents, and to do so regarding a country such as Brazil, where the spread of the gospel would certainly encounter strong opposition, would jeopardize both the work and workers. In his reply to Mr Baird the doctor acknowledged the dire necessity of taking the gospel to Brazil, but experience in Madeira had taught him the need for prudence when undertaking such a task.

The spiritual needs of Brazil constituted God's call to service in that field. Humbly and with a deep sense of their own inadequacy, Dr Kalley and his wife accepted the challenge and began preparations to sail for Brazil.

Part II
Brazil

'Leaving Britain would have been unbearable but for the feeling that it was to carry words of peace from God to rebel creatures and with the hope of seeing fruit for our trials and labours for ever. The object in view is worth labouring for, suffering for, and it is worth spending life in pursuit of it.'

(Dr Kalley's diary, 8 April 1855, on leaving Southampton for Brazil.)

'May it please Almighty God to enable me to speak during the time he may allow me this year, to the honour and glory of Jesus Christ, and that I may understand that I am a member of his body – in vital union with the Lord of glory – guided by the Holy Spirit and having always before me what he says:

a.   'Without me ye can do nothing;

b.   'Ask of me and I will give you all that is needed;

c.   'For whosoever shall give a cup of water in my name shall not lose his reward;

d.   'I will say unto him, well done good and faithful servant, enter into the joy of thy Lord.'

(Dr Kalley – New Year Resolution 1867.)

10.
The choice is made

In the turbulent period of Brazil's independence in the year 1822, the whole future of the country seemed to depend on one word, *'fico'* – 'I will remain'. It was the decision of the future emperor, D. Pedro I, not to return to Portugal as he had been ordered to do by his father in Lisbon, D. Joao VI, but to remain in Brazil and lead the nation on to full independence and liberty. He declared, 'Since it is for the good of all and the happiness of the nation, tell the people I will remain.' Thirty-three years later, 1855, the same word, this time in the plural, *'ficaremos'* was made by those who were to lead Brazilians into a gospel-inspired spiritual liberty.

Arrival in Rio

At daybreak on 10 May 1855 the 'colossus of the sea', the paddle steamer *Great Western*, famed as winner of the Blue Riband for the fastest crossing of the Atlantic in 1838, in fifteen days, dropped anchor in Guanabara Bay, Rio de Janeiro. The journey from Southampton had taken a month. On board were Dr and Mrs Kalley. As dawn broke and the ship slowly passed the Sugar Loaf mountain, guardian of the bay, the sight that greeted them fully justified what Miss Marianne North – a much-travelled English lady – had written: 'The beautiful bay of Rio which certainly is the most lovely landscape in the world; even Naples and Palmero must be content to hold second place in point of natural beauty ...' The scene must have been for them as awe-inspiring as it had been for Miss North and for travellers down through the centuries since the Portuguese first discovered the Bay early in the sixteenth century. To the south the heavily wooded Serra do Mar, with the main peaks of Gavea and Corcovado glowing in the early morning sunshine; to the north and east the Serra dos Orgãos ('Organ Mountains') with the 'sleeping giant' clearly outlined by the skyline of peaks; beyond the first range of these mountains that remarkable pinnacle of granite pointing heavenwards, O Dedo de Deus – the 'Finger of God'. And the bay itself, with its numerous inlets and sprinkling of islands, a landscape indeed second to none in natural beauty. On the southern shore, hemmed in on the narrow strip between the mountains and the sea, Rio de Janeiro or, to give it its full title, São Sebastião do Rio de Janeiro (St Sebastian of the January River); and, on the northern shore, bordering a long stretch of beautiful sands, the town of Niteroi completed the picture. It was the dawn of a new day for the Kalleys as also for Brazil.

Then came the excitement of disembarkation – the vociferous gesticulating hordes of would-be baggage handlers, hotel agents, hucksters of an infinite variety of wares, all clamouring for attention and all manning a seething fleet of small boats, bobbing up and down in the swell and jostling one another to find a vantage-point near the vessel. The Kalleys had an advantage: they could speak the language, Portuguese, and so haggle directly with the aspiring helpers. Seasoned travellers though they were, they always found it a strain to oversee the unloading of their baggage and finally descend the ship's ladder and clamber aboard a launch.

What a crowd awaited them on shore at the point of landing! The French artist Jean Baptiste Debret, commissioned to paint street scenes in Rio in 1816 by the newly-arrived Portuguese King, João VI, has vividly portrayed the crowd congregating at the landing site. Slaves are much in evidence: negroes going about their humble tasks of carrying burdens, running errands or just loafing about; negresses selling sweetmeats or drinks from clay pots; also soldiers from the nearby barracks on duty or standing chatting and citizens going about their business. The picture gives a good cross-section of the population the Kalleys would see the day they landed. There was the preponderance of African slaves, at least two to one in relation to other inhabitants, giving the impression that Brazilians are more African than South American! That is only true in part since the genuine Brazilian is a mixture of Portuguese and rain-forest Indian and, with the arrival of slaves, that strain was added to the race. Although the Kalleys would not notice evidence of this in the city itself, the government had recently embarked on an immigration policy, attracting German and Swiss settlers to occupy the vast areas of, as yet, uncultivated land. The authorities termed this influx of Europeans the 'bleaching process'!

Rio de Janeiro

Immediately on landing the Kalleys hired a conveyance and toured the city in the hope of finding a suitable residence which they could rent. Not being successful they settled in a hotel named the Pharoux on the seafront, not far from the point of disembarkation. The excitement and stress of the morning had drained their energies. From the anchorage of the *Great Western* out in the bay the city had looked so beautiful, but a close-up view as they toured the streets gave a different and unpleasing impression. They were disillusioned – things were not as they had expected them to be. The city was disappointing, although the site was attractive with its four hills and intervening valleys and low-lying areas. Everywhere there were churches and unsightly monastic buildings belonging to the various religious orders. They capped the hills and spilled over into the squares below. Priests, monks and friars were much in evidence on the streets. The streets themselves were narrow, badly paved, if paved at all, and at night badly lit, as gas lamps which had been installed that year were not sufficiently numerous to give a good light. Sewers were nonexistent, the centre of the street being an open sewer clogged with stinking filth awaiting the rains to wash it away and cleanse the whole city. There were no really fine houses or public buildings. Even the palace was drab and uninteresting. The Jesuits had been expelled from Brazil and the government had taken over their buildings to house its various departments. As one Brazilian remarked, they got their public buildings on the cheap!

There were terraced houses of two or three storeys with façades of beautiful Portuguese tiles, wrought-iron balconies and wooden shutters, but the majority of the houses were low, one-storied dwellings. The Kalleys could not find one house to suit their needs. And as for the city itself they fully agreed with what a Brazilian writer of the period had to say: 'The town is an immense ugly village, lacking in amenities and swept by epidemics.' It lacked the dignity of a capital city.

To stay – or not to stay

Once settled in their hotel room Dr and Mrs Kalley took stock of the situation – the excessively moist heat, the flies and the stench which even pervaded their room. They later discovered that the hotel was situated close to the place where refuse and sewerage was tipped over the sea-wall by slaves. All combined it was too overpowering for words. They sat in silence each knowing what the other was thinking: 'Why are we here? Can we ever become acclimatized to this heat? Really, we have no reason to stay here. We are unknown; no one knows us and we know no one, so why stay? The ship is still in port. Why not slip back on board and do the Lord's work in more pleasant surroundings? There is an abundance of Portuguese colonies awaiting the gospel!' The doctor looked at his wife quizzically. He had made up his mind but not without a clash of conflicting thoughts. To what conclusion had she come? Quietly and decisively she declared, '*Ficaremos*' – 'we will stay'. The crisis was passed. They were at one in their decision to stay, a decision they were never to regret.

And yet, even after the momentous decision was made, doubts as to the wisdom of it still perturbed their thoughts. The doctor wrote in his diary, 'Sarah restless. God, show us what to do! If we turn and give up work here, it will likely discourage Christian effort for Brazil more than ever. If we turn now we will lose, and will deserve to lose, the respect and confidence of Christian men, and be regarded as speculative adventurers – all influence lost everywhere. That, therefore, must not be thought of unless God, in his providence, give some clear indication, commanding us to go. Though it should cost life and all – *we must stay*.'

Reflections on their journey

The Kalleys, then, did stay on. Had they had time for reflection in the bustle of those first days, they would have recalled that they had had a very pleasant journey over from Britain. They had had a good send-off, friends and relatives wishing them God-speed. The ship had called at Lisbon, but the highlight of the trip had come when they cast anchor in the Bay of Funchal, Madeira. Dr Kalley's sister Jane and her husband Dr Miller were resident in Madeira, and had entertained them for the day. They had visited old scenes – the house in Santa Luzia where the doctor had lived, the house further up the hill where he had found refuge when fleeing from the mob, the British Consulate, the route his bearers had followed when they carried him by hammock to safety. The one regret Mrs Kalley had was that she did not see the prison where her husband had spent six months in detention.

The boat had also put in to Recife, Pernambuco and Salvador, Bahia, but they did not go ashore. They were introduced to Brazil and its people when several Brazilian senators had embarked, *en route* for the new parliamentary session in Rio de Janeiro. They were very distinguished politicians – Francisco Xavier Paes Barreto, president of the State of Paraiba; Francisco Gonçalves Martins, Viscount of São Lourenço; Domingos Souza Leão, Baron of Vila Bela; João Lustoso Cunha, Marquis of Paranagua, besides other lesser-known figures. Dr Kalley conversed with these men and found at least two of them to be very friendly indeed. One of them, Viscount of São Lourenço, had the reputation of being 'one of the greatest talents in the empire' and with him the doctor talked freely and at length. He became a firm friend of the doctor's and proved to be of great assistance to Richard Holden, a missionary in Bahia. On the decks of the *Great Western* the Kalleys had their first taste of Brazilian culture.

Settling in

They found it harder to settle in to life in Rio than they had anticipated. Not even their experiences in the Near East and the West Indies had prepared them for the cultural shock that they experienced in the Brazilian capital. The heat, smells, predominance of African slaves, transit of horses, mules, public conveyances, carriages, pedestrians from every walk of life, thronging the narrow streets – it was all bewildering, disappointing, disheartening. They had letters of introduction to various people, both British and Brazilian, which they delivered personally. Each one of these new acquaintances was presented with a gold watch, brought specially from England for the purpose! In this way they got to know one who was to become an intimate friend and a great help to them: Dr José Martins da Cruz Jobim, a senator, doctor to the emperor, director of medical institutions. They were to learn a feature of Brazilian culture – the importance of having friends in high places. A Brazilian will do anything for a friend!

11.
The 'land of the Christless cross'

Stay the Kalleys did for twenty-one years, and in staying they were to accomplish what others in the past had failed to do, that is, to plant the cross of the living Christ in the 'land of the Christless cross' – and that on a sure and lasting foundation.

A 'Christless cross'? In order to understand what is meant by that it is necessary to delve briefly into history and, in doing so, to digress from the Kalley story.

For 500 years, from the eighth to the thirteenth centuries, the Moors occupied Portugal and the cross was subservient to the crescent. With their defeat and final expulsion the victorious cross became as much a national symbol and rallying point as the royal standard itself. This cross, however, was hewn from extra-biblical material, i.e. ecclesiastical tradition. Priests and monks shaped it and instilled its image into the minds of the people. Christ was on the cross in the form of a crucifix, but as a pathetic, dying figure, capable of arousing only pity. Christ as a living reality was unknown. Beyond the cross, in the minds of the people, he did exist in heaven, but as a remote, shadowy figure, shrouded in glory and unapproachable except through the mediation of Mary and the saints. Mary was a reality – her image in an infinite variety of guises was to be found everywhere. So also the saints, those who through accumulated merit had earned for themselves canonization. Their images and icons were commonplace. In vain the Catholic Church taught that images were to be venerated and God only to be adored; the people rendered to Mary and the saints the adoration due to God alone. True, Christ was said to be present in the mass, but only through the transubstantiation of the wafer and wine; these became the body

and blood of the Lord 'just as they exist in heaven'. The cross
with its trappings was therefore stripped of any reality as
regards the living Lord. The cross was not his.

The cross implanted

The aim of the Portuguese in undertaking their great voyages
of discovery in the sixteenth century was not merely to find
and claim new territories for the Crown, but it was also to
implant the cross there too. A voyage of discovery was a
crusade. The militancy so characteristic of the crescent was
now the dominant factor of the uplifted cross. The eight-
pointed cross of the Knights Templar, now the military order
of Christ, gleamed bright red on the sails of the caravels that
carried the explorers. A fanatical faith in the cross was burning in the souls of these men, and they believed that the same
credulity must be infused into the souls of the pagans they
conquered, even at the point of the sword.

When, in 1500, Pedro Alves Cabral sailed from the Tagus
at the head of a small fleet of assorted vessels commissioned
to found a Portuguese colony in Calcutta, wind and current
carried him to an unknown coast, later discovered to be
Brazil. True to his faith, he called the first mountain to appear
on the horizon Mount Paschoal, and the land he discovered
the 'Land of the Holy Cross'. In the expedition there were
monks as well as soldiers. The Indians who witnessed the arrival of the adventurers on the beach at Porto Seguro ('Safe
Port') saw strange things that day – ships, white men, armour
and weapons, but strangest of all was the ceremony they saw
enacted immediately after the landing. Men clothed differ-
ently from the rest made a mound of stones and on it erected
a great wooden cross. They intoned strange words and, while
everyone knelt, uplifted the wafer and the chalice. So
entranced were the aboriginals that during the ritual they
imitated the strangers' every action, kneeling and rising, raising their arms in unison with them. Impressed, the Francis-
cans wrote enthusiastically in letters despatched to Lisbon
that these children of the forest would soon be converted to
the new faith. The Indians were to become familiar with the
priest, the cross, the mass, as also with the images of the

saints, pilgrimages and vows – all the trappings of the medieval Roman Catholic Church. Against these things, extraneous to the Bible, the Reformers had inveighed as being of no value to the soul.

The Indians did not prove to be as malleable as the friars thought; they would become 'Christians', but under duress. Inevitably they would graft on to the Roman Catholic dogmas and practices their own paganism. This also the African slaves were to copy, only to a much greater extent. These were baptized in the sea when they embarked in Africa and branded on the chest with a cross, in order that they might be sold as 'Christians' on arrival at the slave markets in Brazil and so fetch a better price. They were forced to kiss the cross, but at heart they remained pagan. Not only were they baptized and given Christian names, but inevitably their gods were also 'baptized' and reincarnated as saints. In the 'Land of the Holy Cross' the cross was not only Christless but ingrained with the ignorance, superstition and idolatry of paganism.

Brazil stood in desperate need of the gospel. In his book *Mansions and Shanties*, Gilberto Freyre, the eminent Brazilian sociologist, writes: 'Nobody today is so deluded as to think that we Brazilians – nearly all of us, even those of São Paulo and Rio Grande do Sul, with our negro cousins – are really a Latin people, and even less strictly Christian ... We are agreed that Catholicism was a powerful factor in the integration of Brazil but a Catholicism which, in its contacts in the Iberian Peninsula with African form of religion, acquires a dark mulatto tinge. Thus it adapted itself to the conditions of life in the tropics and to our people of hybrid origin. The doors of the shrines opened wide to admit African idols disguised as St Cosmo and St Ammian, coal-black St Benedicts and St Iphigenias, dark-hued Madonnas of the Rosary, coloured saints who took their place beside fair St Anthonys, golden-locked cherubs, in a fraternization that outdid that of humans. Saints and angels, traditionally blond, were forced to imitate the people, becoming like them, the relatives of blacks and mulattos. In the hands of our image-makers even Our Lady took on mulatto traits, sometimes putting on flesh and acquiring the breasts of a black mother. And, the most popular image of Christ in Brazil is that of a dark, paled Jew, with black or, at most brown, hair and beard and not blond

The statue of Christ the Redeemer on the Cocovado mountain overlooking Rio de Janeiro

like the historical or orthodox Northern European represen-
tation of the Redeemer. It may be that if the priest had
insisted on imposing on the people golden-haired or blond
saints, they would have estranged a large number of Brazilians from Catholicism, and there might have grown up
around the altar and the saints the atmosphere of coolness
and indifference as around the throne of blond emperors and
regents. There is basis for the truth in the rather far-fetched
allegation that the first emperor lost his throne because he
was not a native-born Brazilian and the second because he
was not a mulatto.' Catholicism had been grafted on to pagan
stock, the latter polluting the former. Dr and Mrs Kalley may
not have been fully aware of all this when they landed, but
they were soon to understand it as they settled down to live in
Brazil.

French exiles bring the gospel

In 1555, exactly 300 years before the Kalleys landed, a group
of French Protestants arrived in the Bay of Guanabara,
seeking asylum from persecution. Admiral Coligny, head of
the Huguenot minority in France and chief martyr on the
night of the Massacre of St Bartholomew, gave them his
blessing and approved of their leader, Villegagnon, a man
whose reputation for daring was established when he ran the
English blockade and carried the young Mary, Queen of
Scots, safely to France. The French took possession of an
island in the bay, fortified it, formed an alliance with the
Tamoio Indians who roamed the shores of the mainland and
succeeded in founding a colony to which they gave the grand-
iose title 'the French Antarctic'. Their intention was to form
a truly Christian community under the pastoral care of ministers from Geneva. In fact, the first date on the calendar of the
Brazilian Evangelical Church is 10 March 1557, the day when
the French pastor Peter Richier conducted a service according to the reformed faith for the first time on Brazilian soil.
The success of the colony was short-lived, since Villegagnon
soon revealed his deep-seated aversion to the faith he had so
enthusiastically espoused when gathering together the expedition in France. He scattered the faithful. Three suffered

martyrdom; they were garrotted and their bodies thrown into the sea. Others escaped by boat, very few eventually finding their way back to France. The Portuguese were already firmly established farther south and north along the coast, and they regarded all Brazilian territory as theirs. Their troops, under the leadership of one of the most famous of Brazil's great figures, Estácio de Sá, expelled the remainder of the French from the bay. A final battle was fought against the Tamoios and won on St Sebastian's Day, and in order to avoid further foreign incursions, Estácio de Sá founded a city there and named it São Sebastião do Rio de Janeiro.

One of the French pastors, known in Brazilian history as João de Boles, found refuge for a short while in São Vicente, the first Portuguese settlement in Brazil, now the port of Santos on the coast near São Paulo. He propagated the gospel so zealously among both Indians and Portuguese that he attracted the hostile attentions of the Jesuits. They effectively silenced his witness by ordering his arrest and after years of imprisonment and suffering had him condemned to death. Anchieta, a Jesuit priest celebrated in Brazilian history as the pacifier of the Indians, claimed to have converted the heretic at last, and fearing that he might recant, himself adjusted the hangman's noose so as to dispatch his victim with the utmost speed. With Bole's death the last remnant of the French Antarctic was wiped out and the first attempt to implant the gospel in Brazil completely frustrated. Mem de Sá, father of Estácio, had the last word: 'The Lord did not want Lutherans and Calvinists planted in this land of Brazil.'

The militant cross had won a battle over biblical truth.

Dutch settlers establish churches

The second attempt to take the gospel to Brazil was made by the Dutch. They, in the early part of the seventeenth century, floated the West India Company, hoping to exploit the wealth of the Americas as the East India Company was doing with marked success in the Orient. Brazil was their first objective. In 1624 they obtained a precarious foothold in Salvador, at that time capital of the colony, but they were forced to withdraw. Six years later they established a bridgehead in

Pernambuco, and from there gradually extended their conquest until they controlled the whole of north-east Brazil. They rebuilt the devastated village of Recife and made it the finest city in the land. In layout and in architectural beauty if far surpassed anything the country had previously known. The Dutch enriched themselves on the sugar plantations and under the wise rule of John Maurice, Prince of Nassau, the colony flourished. The prince sought to educate the people by bringing over from Europe men of letters, artists and others and, contrary to the custom of the times, allowed full religious liberty. The Dutch were of the reformed faith, and established numerous churches for both the Dutch and Brazilian communities. The church was missionary-minded and planned to take the gospel to the Indian tribes. These plans never matured, for after a prolonged struggle the Brazilians, a guerrilla band consisting of Portuguese colonists, African slaves and Indians, together with numerous half-breeds, succeeded in driving out the invaders. The campaign is known in history as the 'Pernambuco Insurrection' and the men who led it – the Indian chief, Camarão, the African, Henrique Dias, the Portuguese Vieira, the Brazilian, Negreiros – are revered as the progenitors of Brazilian independence, since they gained the victory alone, with no help from Lisbon.

Thus in 1654 the second attempt to spread the gospel in Brazil failed. Once more, the Christless cross had won another battle over the biblical truth of the gospel. All traces of the reformed faith were systematically eradicated: Dutch Protestant churches were converted to Catholic use; Indians influenced by the gospel were forced back into the Catholic fold; nothing remained to indicate that for almost thirty years the gospel had been faithfully proclaimed in north-east Brazil.

British trade-links

For the next century and a half Brazil was a closed land. All invaders had been expelled – the French, who had re-established themselves in the north and founded the town of São Luiz de Maranhão, and even the British, who had built two forts in the extreme north. The Portuguese colonized all strong points on the coast and effectively closed the land to traders and heretics. Only through Lisbon was contact with the outer world maintained. Any stray foreigner who found his way to Brazil was summarily dealt with: he was condemned by the Inquisition and burned as a Jew. There was, however, one interesting exception.

In 1703 England, as an ally of Portugal, obtained a concession, by the Treaty of Methuan, for four British families to reside and trade in the three principal cities – Bahia, Rio and Recife. Change was imminent, however; the king, Don Joao VI and his court, at British instigation and under British protection, fled from Lisbon to Brazil from the dangers of the Napoleonic invasion of the Iberian Peninsula. It was then, in 1808, that Brazilian ports were thrown open to world trade and direct commerce with other countries established. The law prohibiting manufacture was revoked and industrial development incremented. The British benefited greatly by these measures. They exploited to the full the new market opened to them. Within a year British merchants were established in the commercial centres and the flow of British goods into Brazil began – iron, glass, china, tea, an endless list. British industry and enterprise followed rapidly – the foundry, railway, sewage systems, gold-mining, shipping, banking, gas and still later the telegraph, the submarine cable and electricity. In every department of Brazilian commercial life British influence made itself felt. In 1881 it was said that England had more trade links with Brazil than with any other country. The Brazilians hold that George Canning (1770-1827), the British statesman and the first to recognize the free states of South America, was the 'godfather' of Brazilian independence, so great was his effort to make it a reality.

Another service the British rendered to Brazil was to identify and make known to the world the country's immense wealth of fauna. Dr G. Gardener, superintendent of the Botanical Gardens in Ceylon, travelled extensively in Brazil from 1836-41 on behalf of Kew and Glasgow. Four years later another Englishman, Dr T. Bridges, while exploring a tributary of the River Marmore, discovered in a quiet pool the most wonderful water lily ever seen. In his excitement he would have plunged into the lake to swim out to the spot where the lily floated, had not the Indian guides restrained him. The pool was infested with alligators, some of which were sunning themselves within a few feet of the flower. Bridges obtained seeds which he carried to Kew. The plants developed, one of which was sent to the hothouses of Chatsworth. The *Victoria Regis* was now known and universally admired. As Gilberto Freyre, renowned Brazilian writer remarks, 'The British have the knack of combining the useful with the beautiful.' He might have added, 'and the pleasurable too', since Britain gave to Brazil its great national sport, football!

Protestantism granted official recognition

There was one major issue which remained outstanding – the question of religious freedom. The British, already well-established in Brazil, and the settlers, principally German and Swiss, invited by the government to occupy and cultivate the vast expanses of the hinterland, demanded to enjoy freedom to worship according to the dictates of their conscience. It was so in the United States, the other developing country, and they held that it must be so in Brazil as well. The Roman Catholic Church opposed such a policy. The British, who formed ever growing enclaves in the big cities, insisted on the right to have Church of England chaplains to minister to their spiritual needs. The opposition of the Catholic hierarchy became tenacious: they were adamant in their refusal to allow a Protestant church to enter Brazil under any pretext whatever. The British finally won their case when a wise old dignitary of the Catholic community unwittingly became their ally. He sagely reminded his fellow clergy that the British fight persistently for a thing until they get it, but once they have it they neglect and forget it. 'Let them have their church, since that is the surest way to make them forget it and never attend its services.'

A treaty was drawn up between the governments of Britain and Brazil by which a chaplaincy was established in each British colony. It was stipulated, however, that the churches were not to have the outward appearance of places of worship – no bell, no steeple, no stained-glass windows and, above all, there must be no attempt to proselytize Brazilians. Later, Lutherans obtained a similar concession to serve the German enclaves entrenched in the southern states of the country. Protestantism had arrived in Brazil but not as a militant force. It had obtained official recognition, but its witness was nullified by the restrictions imposed upon it. As a result of these deadening influences neither the Church of England nor the Lutheran Church played any part in the evangelization of Brazil. It was still the 'Land of the Holy Cross'; the domineering influence of that cross remained unchallenged. It had weathered the storms of centuries, but its greatest challenge was at hand. It was appropriate that citizens of Britain, the country that had benefited most from Brazil's open-trade policy, Dr and Mrs Kalley, should present that challenge. They were to bring to Brazil that which, in the last analysis, had made Britain great – the Bible, the gospel, the living Christ.

12.
An open door

What was the Brazilian setting into which Dr Kalley introduced the gospel? As to the clergy, the number of native clergy was reduced to a minimum: monasteries were empty and there were practically no recruits for the priesthood. Those who were in holy orders were, for the most part, lax in morals and in doctrine, and entirely lacking in apostolic vision and zeal. City churches had the priority and attracted the few priests that were available, while the scattered communities in the vast hinterland had to content themselves with very occasional visits from the priests, usually at some *festa* of the local saint. Simony – the buying or selling of the spiritual or sacred – was rampant, too.

In the absence of the priest the people themselves sought to supply their own spiritual needs. One more religiously minded than the rest would lead the community in the recital of prayers, the *novena*. Kidder described the scene vividly when he stayed at a farm: 'During the evening half an hour was devoted to prayers. I saw a number of coloured folk enter a room, and they saluted one another with hands crossed on the breast: "Praise be to our Lord Jesus Christ." After that they began to intone the prayers. They would be kneeling before the oratory, duly decorated with tinsel and lit by candles. In this case the one who led the prayers was a layman, an old coloured man.' Kidder continues: 'These gatherings of slaves at night, or sometimes in the early morning, are common. The pleasure the slaves get out of such occasions, very frequently – since saints' days are so many – constitutes without doubt a powerful lenitive to their servile condition.'

Such gatherings in which the laity played so prominent a part, and the love of singing, prepared the way for the *culto evangélico* – the evangelical meeting. These people were schooled by their upbringing to gather together, with one of their own number as leader. Hence they did not find it strange to gather round the Bible in a home and listen to the exposition ministered by one of themselves. One thing is certain, they learned more of the truth by hearing the Word of God expounded by a humble believer than from all the accumulated years of the most punctilious observance of saints' days, or even from the exacting ceremonies of Holy Week!

Official tolerance

In official circles the spirit of tolerance prevailed. It was fashionable to be tolerant. Protestant nations, England and Prussia had dethroned Napoleon and secured the Portuguese throne for the Bragança family. England had contributed decisively to Brazilian independence. Protestantism, in theory at least, if not in practice, was in the ascendency. Many of the relatively few native clergy were liberal, as Kidder discovered on his colportage travels. They professed themselves to be disciples of Jansenius, a Dutch theologian, who expounded fully and freely the doctrines of St Augustine. His dogma became a basic study in the seminaries of Rio and Recife. The clergy trained in these schools were favourable to the wide distribution of the Word of God and readily undertook to give away copies of the Scriptures that Kidder left with them. Unfortunately there was a strong admixture of foreign priests and prelates who were fanatical defenders of the Tridentine dogmas and, as such, tenaciously opposed to Bible reading, especially by plebeians, and they were in the majority!

Brazil's leading politician, Padre Feijó, was typical of the liberal native clergy. He was a priest and an intellectual who began his political career as a deputy and rose to be Minister of Justice and a senator. He reached the height of his career when, in 1837, he became Regent during the minority of the young Emperor Dom Pedro II. As Jansenius had advocated Feijó aimed at reforming the Catholic Church in Brazil and by doing so raising the spiritual level of the country as a whole. He sought authority for priests to marry and in that way sort out their domestic tangles. He even suggested to the Marquis of Barbacena, then in London, that he invite the Moravian brethren to come to Brazil to do what they had done in other countries – evangelize and teach the people. Above all, he envisaged a break with Rome and the establishment of a Brazilian Catholic Church similar to what Henry VIII had done in England. Kidder was a close friend of the Regent and very rightly sympathized with his aspirations.

The emperor's attitude

Two other factors that weighed heavily in favour of the gospel were the attitude of the young emperor and the immigration policy of his government. Dom Pedro II had been proclaimed emperor when his father was deposed. He was born in Brazil, his people accepted him as a true Brazilian and, under the tutelage of Feijó, his love for his people and his country developed. He was a wise, tolerant ruler, interested in the welfare of the nation. He professed himself to be Roman Catholic but disliked Rome intensely. His whole-hearted sympathy was with the movement that sought to break away from the Vatican and so free the church for its true mission, that of ministering to the spiritual needs of the people. He was essentially a student, given to the study of the arts and sciences, and that may have contributed to his utter disregard for the message of the state church. He believed in a social gospel, in a church that would uphold the government in its endeavour to combat social evils and raise living standards. Had he been free to act independently he would have transformed every priest and friar into a teacher or tutor, and every army officer into a scientist or an engineer.

In her book of travels and paintings *Vision of Eden*, Miss Marianne North writes of a visit she paid to the emperor in Rio de Janeiro in 1873: 'The Emperor was a man who would be worth some to know, even if he were the poorest of private gentlemen; he is eminently a gentleman, and full of information and general knowledge on all subjects. He lives more the life of a student than that to which ordinary princes condemn themselves. He gives no public entertainment, but on certain days he and the Empress will receive the poorest of their subjects who like to take their complaints to him. He kindly gave me a special appointment in the morning and spent more than an hour examining my paintings and talking them over, giving me the names and qualities of different plants which I myself did not know. He then took the whole mass – no small weight – in his arms and carried them in to show the Empress, telling me to follow. She also was very kind with a sweet, gentle manner, and both had learned since their journey to Europe (of which they never tired of talking) to shake hands in the English manner! They both had prematurely white hair, brought on by the trouble of losing their daughter and the miserable war with Paraguay. On my second visit to the palace the Emperor was good enough to show me his museum in which there is a magnificent collection of minerals.' Four years later, shortly after Miss North had returned from a visit to the Far East, the emperor paid a visit to her flat in London. 'He looked at all my curiosities and paintings and told me about my different friends in his country, forgetting nobody that he thought I was interested in, with his marvellous memory.'

The emperor, with his more enlightened ministers, saw the need for immigration and encouraged it. A few days before Dr Kalley arrived the emperor, in his speech from the throne at the opening of the Third National Assembly stated: 'My government will give special attention to the promoting of colonization on which the future of the country depends.' He looked to Protestant countries to meet Brazil's greatest need – more people – and took as an example the wise colonial policy of the United States with its freedom of worship and of conscience, together with equal civil and political rights.

Kidder was correct in his summing up of the situation in Brazil as he understood it – that in no other Roman Catholic country in the world was so tolerant a spirit to be found. Even so, although Dr Kalley could say with Paul, 'A wide door for effective work has been opened for me', he could also add, 'and there are many adversaries.'

13.
Gernheim

The Kalleys moved to a hotel away from the sea-front, the Hotel dos Estrangeiros in a central location, the square known as the Praça do Catete. There the atmosphere was more salubrious and life more tolerable. Their chief concern was to find a suitable house. It needed to be appropriate to their social status, to be in one of the healthier parts of the town, to have a room large enough to hold meetings and last, but not least, to be easily accessible. The Kalleys toured the town in the hope of finding the ideal residence, but they were unsuccessful in their search, even after weeks of persistent endeavour. Twice they thought that they had found the right house, but each time were thwarted. It was all exceedingly frustrating. The doctor noted in his diary: 'Sarah dispirited. We seem to be doing nothing for ourselves or others, but are torpid and useless, having no intercourse with anybody. Might be doing more at home ... Memory, heart and judgement all seem reeling, yet how great my privilege compared with the most successful merchants – English or Brazilian.'

Naturally they desired to remain incognito, fearing that the doctor's experience in Madeira might prove prejudicial to the work they hoped to do in Brazil, but almost immediately he was recognized and hailed by one of his old patients from Madeira! The reality could not be disguised, the 'Wolf from Scotland' had arrived in Brazil!

Petropolis

The Kalleys were assured by Brazilian acquaintances that what they had failed to find in Rio they would certainly find in the neighbouring town of Petropolis, situated high in the Organ Mountains. Rio de Janeiro was not a healthy place in which to live: sanitation was non-existent, water was scarce, the atmosphere heavy and humid, and with the coming of the hot season, from October to March, it would become stifling. Yellow fever and typhoid claimed endless victims, especially among British residents. The headstones in the British cemetery in the Gambôa district of the city testified eloquently to the danger of residing in such an unhealthy climate.

Petropolis had been purpose-built a few years previously as a summer residence for the emperor and his court. Its situation in the mountains behind Rio was ideal: delightful climate, beautiful surroundings, and situated on the main trail between Minas Gerais, with its wealth of gold and precious stones, and the capital city. The lay-out of the town was spacious, free from the filth so characteristic of Rio, and more like a capital city than Rio. The government departments were housed in well-designed buildings; the emperor's palace was very imposing; the aristocracy had built for themselves palatial residences. It was a pleasant town in which to fix residence. It was there, too, that the impact of the government's immigration policy was apparent – German and Swiss labourers congregated there, living in rows of humble cottages. There was even a German Lutheran church, a concession to the newcomers.

The Kalleys finally heeded the advice given by Brazilian friends and made an exploratory visit to Petropolis. They were fortunate since the railway *en route* for the town had just been built – the first railway in Brazil. The journey was by no means easy, as Miss Marianne North discovered some twenty years later. She wrote, 'I crossed from "Prainha" on the Bay by boat to Maua where a train was waiting to take us over the marsh to the foot of the Petropolis hills. At last we reached a more healthy-looking region and stopped at "Raiz da Serra" (Foot of the Mountain), where I was put in a carriage with three Brazilians and conveyed up the ten miles of zig-zag road, dragged by four mules, who kept up a continuous trot, the rise of three thousand feet being well graduated. Two more miles at full gallop took us down hill to Petropolis.' A hectic journey, as murals of that period depict the road as being crowded – carts, pack mules, slaves on foot, carriages of the aristocracy – complete with postillions and outriders! Miss North was not impressed with the town, likening it to a 'second-class German watering-place', but she only stayed two days and, according to her own confession, they were days 'of rain, of cold, of loneliness; I worked, walked, soaked and froze'. Later she was to revise her opinion in better weather and more pleasant company.

In Petropolis Dr and Mrs Kalley found exactly what they had been looking for – a suitable house, situated in spacious grounds dotted by the cottages of German labourers. It was the home of the American ambassador, and shortly to be vacated. The name of the property was Gernheim, 'home well-beloved', indicative of its pleasing aspect. Since occupancy would only be in October, the Kalleys continued to reside in Rio until the end of July and then took temporary accommodation in a hotel in Petropolis.

When choosing this town as a place in which they could begin their missionary labours, they were undoubtedly influenced by the presence of so many Protestant Germans. To quote from the diary, 'Probably there will never be so large a group of imported Protestants, nor circumstances so promising for the truth to be propagated at the Court [Rio-Petropolis area] of this degraded country.'

They became acquainted with many people; their social status and their fluency in Portuguese and German, as well as English, gave them a distinct advantage. There was, however, one serious drawback – the upper-class Brazilian was suspicious of them. Rumours were spread by the Madeirans of social standing that the doctor had been expelled from Madeira as an 'undesirable', a trouble-maker. Dr Kalley was first and foremost a missionary, an ambassador for Christ, with a unique gift for personal evangelism. With the greatest of ease and without causing embarrassment he could 'converse' the gospel, and he did so in any and every circumstance. As to a more public ministry he was cautious in his approach. His experiences in Madeira had taught him the dangers of confrontation with the authorities, whether ecclesiastical or civil and so, at this early stage in his ministry, he avoided holding formal preaching services.

Small beginnings

Brazil in all its vastness and dire need lay open before them, but now that they were settled how would they begin their mission? They began just where they were, in the situation in which they found themselves. The children of German-Swiss Protestant families, as also those of the British and American, needed a Sunday School where they could learn Bible stories. A few days after their arrival, on 19 August, Mrs Kalley gathered together the children of the American ambassador and those of an English family, in a room in Gernheim, kindly lent to them by the ambassador, and told them the story of Jonah.

Just as the mighty Amazon has its source in an insignificant spring high in the Peruvian Andes, so the mighty river of living waters that now flows so freely through Brazil traces its source to that little gathering in Petropolis. The Kalleys' mission to Brazil had begun. From that Sunday the school grew, and once the Kalleys took possession of their new home, it followed an established pattern. First the German-speaking children met at three o'clock; later the Portuguese-Brazilian scholars gathered and, finally, the English and American. Dr Kalley, too, was not idle. He gathered together in his home a group of men for Bible Study every Sunday afternoon and, still later in the day, a group of 'negroes'. These would be the African slaves whom the culture of that time did not permit to sit with their masters. Even in the Roman Catholic Church racial distinctions were strictly adhered to, a different church for each status – whites, negroes, mulattos. In later years, when the evangelical churches were established these distinctions would disappear. In Christ Jesus all are one.

At Gernheim family worship was held daily. The three servants, two German maids and a Portuguese gardener, attended these daily prayers. Thus a lead was given for others to follow. In the pioneer stage of the work family worship in the homes of believers would be one of the principal means of propagating the gospel. Believers were taught: 'Invite your friends and neighbours to attend the singing of hymns, the reading of the Bible and prayers in your home.'

14.
'Come over, and help us'

Dr Kalley fully realized that a well-established missionary base in Rio de Janeiro was essential in order that the good news might irradiate throughout Brazil. He knew that other workers were necessary, as he himself, from his home in Petropolis, could never begin a work in Rio, and neither was it expedient that he should do so in the situation in which he found himself. After leaving the United States he had written a pastoral letter to the churches in Illinois, exhorting them to be ready always to preach the gospel in Portuguese-speaking colonies in any part of the world.

Now, at the beginning of 1856, an urgent invitation was sent to three of these Madeiran families to come to his aid in Brazil. Like the Lord himself, he summoned men from the ordinary walks of life to go out and preach the gospel.

Instant response

There was an instant, but unexpected response to Dr Kalley's letter to the Madeiran believers in Illinois. An Englishman, William Drayton Pitt, who as a boy had been in Mrs Kalley's Bible Class in Torquay and had emigrated to the United States, had been in contact with the Madeirans resident in Illinois. He answered the appeal and arrived from New York in December 1855. His arrival created a problem for Mrs Kalley as her class-consciousness was still much in evidence. She objected to having William Pitt, a young man of humble origin and a carpenter by trade, sit at the same table with her and her husband. Dr Kalley, however, overruled her objections and received Pitt as an honoured guest. Mrs Kalley learned that day some of the implications of all believers being 'one in Christ Jesus'!

Then trouble came from an unexpected quarter. An epidemic of cholera which was sweeping through the country at that time had reached Petropolis and assumed alarming proportions. A few days after his arrival Pitt caught the disease and for two days his life hung in the balance. He recovered and shortly afterwards found employment in Rio in the Naval Dockyard, as a carpenter. In this way he not only supported himself but began the process of integration into Brazilian life.

The doctor, for his part, decided to offer his services to the health authorities and was duly authorized to treat those suffering from this plague. His medical experiences in Madeira were relived. He concentrated his attention on the poor, on those who would have died not only from the disease but more so from neglect. He was the 'good doctor' once more. Although he treated the wealthy when called to do so, poor and rich alike were dealt with in the same sensitive way. As in Madeira, so in Brazil, he never treated a case without prayer and the ministry of comfort and strength through the Scriptures. One casualty was a grievous loss to him: his old gardener succumbed to cholera. He had been a faithful attendant at family prayers in his employer's home and had professed conversion, and he died firm in the faith, calling on the name of the Lord.

The cost of the call

The doctor had been specific in his invitation to the believers in the United States, naming three men to come with their respective families – Francisco da Gama, Francisco de Souza Jardim and Manuel Fernandes. The decision for them to accept the challenge was not an easy one. It constituted a costly sacrifice to uproot themselves yet again so soon after settling in Illinois. They had lost their all in Madeira, then suffered hard labour on the plantations of the West Indies, and now, once more, were being called upon to leave all for the

sake of the gospel. It would mean exchanging their newly
found freedom for the restrictions, persecutions and fanatical
intolerance prevalent in Brazil.

Their letters in reply to the invitation reflect their thoughts.
Francisco da Gama wrote in April 1856 that he was selling off
what he possessed in Springfield in readiness for the journey
to Rio de Janeiro. He added: 'We received your invitation
calling us to come to you over there, and I was pleased to hear
your voice calling me to such a precious task. I have always
wished to work for my Saviour.'

In his letter Francisco de Souza Jardim is more explicit:
'When Gama received your letter I had already bought a plot
of land and built a wooden house where I and my family were
already living. Your letter invited three families to come to
Brazil, and should none of them wish to accept the invitation,
you asked that the letter be destroyed. My wife summed up
the difficulties: the children, the move to another land, the
long journey, a foreign country, the uncertainties. But I saw
the Lord pointing me to the way. I told my wife that if we did
not go then all the pleasure in life would be lost. We prayed
together and asked the Lord to make clear his will. In a short
time we agreed to accept the invitation. We have dealt with
business matters and are ready to journey.'

The helpers from Madeira

The story of Francisco de Souza Jardim's conversion testifies
to the fact that Dr Kalley's work in Madeira did not finish
when he was expelled from Funchal in 1848. Jardim was there
on that memorable day in August when the city was in uproar,
although he played no active part in the persecution of the
believers. Shortly afterwards a maidservant in the household
in which he was employed urged him to accompany her to a
clandestine Bible Study held in the humble cottage of a farm
labourer. He continued to attend these gatherings and, in the
measure in which he learned the truths of the gospel, he conveyed them enthusiastically to others. Dr Miller, resident in
Madeira, baptized Jardim. So zealous a new convert could
not escape persecution and his continuance in Madeira

became untenable. On Dr Miller's advice he emigrated to the United States and joined his fellow-Madeirans there, and in 1854 came to know Dr Kalley personally.

Jardim and his friends left Baltimore on 7 June and arrived in Brazil two months later. On arrival in Rio they were met by William Pitt and he soon had them settled in a house he had rented in Rua da Boa Vista. As soon as news of their arrival reached Dr Kalley he went down to Rio from Petropolis and that night he and they, ten in all, celebrated the Lord's Supper with 'gladness and singleness of heart, praising God'.

Jardim found work immediately in the Naval Dockyard. Francisco da Gama, who had no profession, was employed by Dr Kalley as a colporteur, selling Scriptures and pamphlets from door to door, while Manuel Fernandes accompanied the doctor back to Petropolis and began work as a colporteur there.

It is interesting to note that when Dr Kalley realized that he must have help if the gospel was to be established in Brazil he did not appeal for a fellow-countryman to be sent out as a missionary. Instead he chose three ordinary men, admirably suited to the task: Portuguese in nationality and culture, converts from Rome, well-experienced in the stratagems of the Roman church, men who had suffered for their faith – Francisco da Gama had been imprisoned in Funchal for several months. Their witness was compelling, whether in family prayers in their homes, in their work as colporteurs or in their daily occupation in the dockyard. They were utterly uninhibited in their testimony to the gospel and fearless too. To them the whole church in Brazil owes a great debt. Laymen, with little or no formal education, but well-schooled in 'the sufferings of Christ for his body's sake, which is the church', they were the foundation stones of that church in Brazil. Regarding them, the Rev. Porto Filho, a leader of the present-day Congregational Church in Brazil writes, 'Gideon had his three hundred, David those who chose to join him; Kalley had these four – Pitt, Gama, Jardim, Fernandes, and their wives, equally dedicated and heroic, having left their all to follow the calling they had received. Honour to them and to the example they gave to the churches that would spring into being through the sowing of the Word, in ground they had watered with their blood, sweat and tears, churches made healthy by the sacrifice they had made for a people in a foreign land.'

In Petropolis, in addition to family prayers and medical treatment of the poor, there was now added colportage work with the arrival of Francisco. Pastoral care by the doctor took on an ever-increasing role, either by letter or by frequent visit to the believers in Rio de Janeiro. One problem which arose was where to find hospitality for the doctor on such visits. Class-consciousness still prevailed and Gama, an erstwhile peasant, would not dare to offer hospitality to someone of the professional class, especially a 'gentleman'! A British friend, a prosperous businessman, placed his home at the doctor's disposal in Tijuca in the foothills. There he would have every comfort and a salubrious climate, but instead he arranged to have a room at Gama's home at his disposal.

A visit to Britain

Then the unexpected happened. News reached them in Petropolis that Sarah's aunt, Mary Morley, was dangerously ill in England, as also grandmother Wilson. They were in a dilemma – should they return to England for a short visit or continue in Petropolis? They decided to go. 'My dear Sarah,' wrote Dr Kalley, 'loved Aunt Mary as a mother, sister, and aunt.' She had in fact been largely responsible for Sarah's upbringing. The Kalleys embarked in Rio in January 1857, having bought return tickets, fully determined to return to Brazil. They arrived in England in time to see Aunt Mary, who died shortly after their arrival. Mrs Wilson, however, recovered from her illness.

While in Britain they took the opportunity to deal with matters affecting their work in Brazil: the supply of Scriptures, tracts, publications, etc. and Mrs Kalley took a series of drawing lessons while in London. By early October though, they were back in Brazil and spent a few days at the Hotel dos Estrangeiros before going up to Petropolis.

Those who honour God...

Mrs Kalley recorded that while in Rio during those few days
her husband chatted with a Mr Clarke, proprietor of a British
shoewear business – Clarke's of Street, Somerset. Sunday
observance was discussed by them. As a result Mr Clarke
advertised that his shops would be closed on Sundays in
future. He fully expected that sales would be seriously
affected but, to his surprise, they actually increased, and continued to increase. New shops were opened in many state
cities of Brazil and they prospered. Dr Kalley believed and
preached that those who honour God, God honours, and Mr
Clarke proved it to be true.

15.
Opposition and encouragement

On their return to Gernheim while, on the one hand the Kalleys continued their consistent, unostentatious witness which brought results, on the other they were still subject to suspicion and harassment. They felt themselves to be under constant surveillance and soon had positive proof that their correspondence was being tampered with – their letters were being censored. It could hardly be otherwise since the Catholic hierarchy had been alerted that 'the Wolf from Scotland' was in residence in Brazil and that constituted a threat to the state religion.

There was a hesitancy on the part of the wealthy and more influential classes to associate with the doctor and his wife. For example, they did not follow the usual Brazilian custom of paying the Kalleys a courtesy call in their home. While not ostracizing them completely they maintained their distance, which was both distasteful and embarrassing to the Kalleys. Neither were relations with the British community on an easy footing. The latter were hard-drinking and worldly with little or no interest in spiritual matters and certainly with no patience for a missionary even though he might be a doctor! Seeing the plight of his fellow-countrymen the doctor sent to England for temperance literature and pledge cards!

First convert

The doctor's approach to his missionary task continued to be cautious and he resolved that he would limit his activities to what was permitted by law. Non-Catholic services could be conducted in German or English to congregations consisting of those nationalities, but there was no law against informal talks in Portuguese on religious matters within the confines of the home. Positive results, however, began to appear. He baptized his first convert, a Portuguese, José Perreira de Souza Lauro.

Although the doctor belonged to the Church of Scotland, and in Madeira was an elder of the Scottish Church there, in Brazil he was to baptize believers only, and that by sprinkling. The Brazilian churches he founded were to follow his lead: only those who professed faith in Christ were baptized and received into church membership. In later years, and after much discussion, members from other Protestant churches who had been baptized in infancy were received into membership without rebaptism, but on one matter Dr Kalley was adamant – converts from Rome must be rebaptized. With this the churches agreed.

Immediately on conversion and baptism José Lauro began to testify to his new-found faith, reading and explaining the Bible to groups of friends and neighbours. He reached out beyond his own circle and sold a Bible to two aristocratic ladies from the emperor's court.

The Fluminense Church

Later, as the hot season of 1858 drew to a close, an epidemic of yellow fever swept through Rio de Janeiro, decimating the population. The doctor gave himself unstintingly to combating the plague, not only tending the sick but also writing and distributing widely a pamphlet advocating prophylactic measures to avoid contamination. The local press praised the doctor for the valuable contribution he made to fighting the dreaded disease.

In Petropolis an 'old soldier' was baptized. The doctor did not, however, attempt to organize the group into a church – they were a 'house group', but on 11 July that year he had the joy of baptizing his first Brazilian convert in Rio de Janeiro, Pedro Nolasco de Andrade. With that baptism he organized the first truly national evangelical church in Brazil. Fourteen members were enrolled consisting of one Brazilian and the remainder either British or Portuguese. It was not long though before two more Brazilians were baptized, Phillip Nery and João Manoel Gonçalves dos Santos, the latter destined to become the first Brazilian pastor of the newly-founded church.

The church was called simply '*Igreja Evangélica*', the name of the region in which it was located being added later – Fluminense. It is the oldest Brazilian Protestant church in the country. It was Dr Kalley's wish that the churches in Brazil should not bear the denominational names nor propagate the denominational distinctions known in the sending countries. His desire was that all should follow the good example set by the *Igreja Evangélica Fluminense*, that is, to the simple title 'Evangelical Church' should be added the name of the town or district in which the church was situated. That plan was carried through in Recife and in the São Paulo area.

The *Igreja Evangélica Fluminense*, so humble in its beginnings, rightly claimed to be in the apostolic succession. Every member was a missionary. A glimpse at the life and labours of those who were baptized during the ministry of Dr Kalley in Brazil reveals this. Their main interest, indeed their exclusive interest, was the extension of the kingdom of Christ. Their names are recorded on the roll of the militant church and their deeds written in heaven; men of humble origin, full of human frailties, beset by problems common to all men, yet men lifted out of obscurity by the Lord who 'chose them and ordained them that they should go forth and bear fruit and that their fruit should abide'.

Persecution of believers

Some of these men were employed, together with Pitt, in the naval dockyards in Rio. During the five years they worked there they were undaunted witnesses for Christ. Their fellow workmen ridiculed them, threw dirty water over them and subjected them to every form of petty persecution. One of the overseers happened to be passing when Jardim was being subjected to some form of horse-play. He intervened and learned from Jardim the reason for such treatment. As a result he gave strict orders that the believers were not to be molested, but to no avail. Serious persecution broke out. One of them, Carvalho by name, was accosted by a beggar as he left work, who asked for 'alms to buy candles for the Holy Trinity'. Carvalho replied that he would willingly give alms to the poor, but since the Holy Trinity created the sun God could not need the light of a puny candle! The beggar's son, a workman in the dockyard, charged Carvalho with having insulted his father and proceeded to thrash him severely. Carvalho, who was a powerfully built man and could easily have crushed his assailant, merely shook him off and went on his way. Two nights later a crowd of workmen attacked the believers. The following Sunday one of them was ordered to attend mass in the Catholic Church, which he refused to do, and the following day all the Protestants received notice to leave employment at the dockyard, on the grounds that they were causing disturbances and were infected with a mania for trying to induce others to accept their views on religion.

In Petropolis, too, opposition hardened. The colporteur, Manoel Fernandes, was arrested and charged with selling books without a licence. In vain he pleaded ignorance as to the necessity for such a licence. He was detained and interrogated, especially as to his relationship with Dr Kalley, but he was eventually released and given the licence.

What brought matters to crisis point, however, was the conversion of two ladies to whom José Lauro had sold a Bible, D. Gabriella Augusta Carneiro Leão, sister of the Marquis of Paraná and of the Baron of Santa Maria, and her daughter Henriqueta. Both had read and studied the Bible assiduously and, as a result, were converted.

The hierarchy of the Catholic Church was incensed: that people from the lower walks of life should be converted was sufficiently alarming, but that prominent and well-connected members of society should abandon the Catholic Church was intolerable. The two ladies professed their reformed faith in January 1859 and in February began to attend the informal gatherings in Gernheim, firstly as spectators, but afterwards as fully integrated members of the fellowship. A few weeks later a pamphlet, violently attacking them, was distributed to the faithful at mass. Dr Kalley was summoned to the office of the chief of police and although granted freedom to propagate his faith, he was prohibited from practising medicine. The papal núncio protested in the strongest terms at this tolerant attitude towards the propagation of the gospel. As a result in June, Brazil's Foreign Minister, Cons. J.N. da Silva Paranhos, summoned Britain's diplomatic representative in Brazil, William Stuart, to his office. He informed Mr Stuart that the president of the state of Rio de Janeiro, Baron de Vila Franca, had formulated a strong case against the doctor: that Dr Kalley preached to the people in general and in particular to his patients and their families; that owing to such illegal practices he had been expelled from Madeira and Trinidad as a disturber of the peace. In all this he maintained that Mrs Sarah Kalley aided and abetted him. Cons. Paranhos stated that the Brazilian constitution was tolerant but not so tolerant as to permit such violations as practised by Dr Kalley.

The doctor and the constitution

Mr Stuart informed the doctor of the situation. In replying to the accusations, Dr Kalley informed Mr Stuart that he had not been the means of the conversion of any Brazilian in Petropolis – the two ladies were already converted when he first knew them; that, while he had held informal gatherings in his own home he had not conducted any formal services in Portuguese. The doctor enclosed with his letter a copy of the findings of three of Brazil's leading jurists, and their answers to eleven questions he had put to them, with a view to clarifying the meaning of the Brazilian constitution. The questions, rhetorical in nature with the exception of the last, yet couched in simple, straightforward terms, progress inexorably towards the climax, the crucial interpretation of Articles 276 and 277 of the Brazilian constitution. These questions, so logical and so persuasive, reveal the doctor's sagacious mentality:

'1.   Brazilian citizens have the right to follow the religion they wish?

'2.   If a citizen consults another as to his faith, has he not the right to receive an explanation?

'3.   Is it a criminal act to counsel such a person?

'4.   Does it matter whether the said person is at home or somewhere else?

'5.   If such a citizen decides to follow a religion other than that of the state, is he a criminal, an apostate, a blasphemer, etc.?

'6.   A fellowship which receives such a person, does it incur a penalty?

'7.   Is it legal for foreigners to hold family worship in their own homes?

'8.   If a Brazilian is present on such an occasion is that a criminal offence?

'9.   If a "foreign" meeting is held in a building that does not have the form of a church, with the doors duly open for anyone who wishes to enter, is that a criminal offence?

'10.   A foreigner, can he be forced to leave his home or be deported, without being formally charged with breaking the law?

'11.   What is the meaning of 'publicly' and ' public meetings' in Articles 276 and 277 of the Brazilian constitution?'

The answers of the three, Drs Joaquim Aurélio Nabuco, Urbano Pessôa de Melo and Caetano Alberto Soares, were unanimous: by the constitution foreign missionaries were free to preach the reformed faith to the people. The considered opinion of these three overturned the interpretation hitherto maintained and adhered to by the official church. It was a great victory: constitutionally the doctor was free to propagate his faith.

Mr Stuart informed Lord Malmesbury at the Foreign Office in London that the Brazilian government had accepted Dr Kalley's explanation, and no further action was called for. Be it said, however, that for his part the doctor had included a veiled threat in his letter that, should he be expelled from the country, he would make widely known, in countries from which Brazil hoped to attract an ever-increasing number of immigrants, that in the matter of religious freedom Brazil was intolerant, in contrast to the United States!

As to practising medicine Dr Kalley, at the suggestion of the authorities, applied to the Faculty of Medicine in Rio for his diploma to be recognized. He was asked to sit an examination and to write a thesis. This he did and was duly registered as a medical practitioner in Brazil in August 1859.

The emperor acts

In spite of the official attitude, however, matters locally did not improve. Two of the doctor's patients died, and the local authorities refused to accept the death certificate signed by the doctor himself. Further troubles for the believers were brewing and the two aristocrats were so harassed that they decided to leave Petropolis. The Kalleys began to feel that they too would have to leave. They were confident, however, that even if they did leave the future of the gospel was assured; the seed sown would continue to bear fruit. Things were at a low ebb when the unexpected happened. The emperor himself intervened!

He called on the Kalleys at Gernheim on 28 February 1860. Unfortunately the doctor was ill, confined to his bed, and unable to see him. Mrs Kalley, however, received him and assured him that her husband would be delighted to receive him once he had recovered. Rumours spread that the emperor had demanded that the Kalleys should leave the country! A few days later Dom Pedro again visited the Kalleys. Ostentatiously he said he wished to converse with the doctor on the Holy Land but in reality he was assuring the couple that he advocated complete religious freedom within the empire. He invited the doctor to the palace to give an illustrated talk on Palestine to the royal family and to the court grandees.

The result of the emperor's friendly gesture was seen immediately. Members of the aristocracy and politicians began to call on the Kalleys at Gernheim, prominent among them Senator Jobim. They were so many that in a letter to her father Sarah Kalley does not even mention them all by name. Many became firm friends of the Kalleys and continued to be so even when they finally moved down to Rio. It is interesting to note that these initial contacts between Don Pedro II and the Kalleys occurred at the time when the papal nuncio arrived back in Petropolis with his retinue – the very man who had exerted all his authority to silence Kalley and to get him expelled!

The new American ambassador, General Watson Webb, was frequently a guest at the Kalleys' hospitable table. A Mr Baillie, of the British Legation, a nephew of the Duke of Manchester and a committed Christian, proved himself to be a loyal helper to the Kalleys in the disturbances they were yet to experience in Rio. Also among their visitors at that time was Prince Albert, Duke of Edinburgh, son of Queen Victoria.

Dr Kalley's new-found friends afterwards played an important role in the fight for religious liberty. Senator José Martins de Cruz Jobim proposed in Parliament that full religious liberty be granted and those who opposed it be charged with criminal offence. In the heated debate that followed he defined his creed: 'I do not believe in anything other than what Christ taught; as to anything else, I have grave doubts, and do not consider it to be of any importance.' Dr Kalley had had many a conversation with Jobim and the results were apparent in the professed creed.

Early in 1860 Gernheim was sold and the Kalleys moved to another rented house called Eyrie. About that time William Pitt's sister, Marianne, arrived in Brazil and became Mrs Kalley's companion.

16.
Outreach from Rio

Salvador

Down the hill in Rio de Janeiro the fledgling Fluminense Church was extending its field of evangelistic activities through the witness of its individual members.

One of the most courageous of these nineteenth-century apostles was Thomas Goulart, a Spaniard by birth and a member of the Fluminense Church. Dr Kalley, now associated in colportage work with the newly arrived agent of the British and Foreign Bible Society, sent Goulart to Salvador, capital of the state of Bahia. Salvador was the 'Athens' of colonial Brazil, the centre of both culture and religion, where there were said to be as many churches in the city itself as there are days in the year. Many of them are gems of baroque architecture, richly adorned, in some cases with gold! The city was Brazil's first capital, the centre of the slave trade and, as such, a place of deeply-rooted traditions and fanatically Roman Catholic. It was to Salvador that Henry Martyn arrived *en route* for India, when his ship was blown off course and needed to take on board fresh supplies before proceeding on its journey. That young missionary found his way into the Convent of St Francis, the treasure of Brazilian colonial architecture, and there, using Latin as a medium, entered into discussion with the friars on the truths of the gospel!

Into this proud, opulent, fanatical city, went the humble colporteur Thomas Goulart some years after Henry Martyn. He was alone. What impact could he have on the life of such a place? And, yet, in a matter of days the city was in an uproar. It was April 1862. The newspapers denounced the presence of the 'false teacher'. The archbishop issued a pastoral to be read in all churches in which he described Goulart as 'a man who goes about selling in the streets false Bibles and booklets about religion, which by the neatness of the printing, the smallness of the volume and its cheapness, are sold with great ease'. Someone took up the cudgels for the new arrival and, signing himself in an article in the press as 'The Friend of the Truth', refuted the bishop's allegations, proving that the Bibles were not false nor the booklets against religion. The Catholic Church replied promptly, threatening with eternal damnation anyone found in possession of a 'false' Bible. Goulart went his way unmoved by the tumult he had caused. He even confronted the priests who had denounced him in the relative safety of their own vicarages. Miraculously he remained unscathed; no one laid violent hands on him. He wrote, 'I give thanks to our King that without the slightest peril he has enabled me to speak freely up till now, in his name, to whites and blacks, to rich and poor, to noble and to artisan, to judges, barons, counsellors and senators.' His pioneer efforts were to bear fruit in later years.

While Goulart was in Salvador, two of the leading citizens advertised in the press that they intended to compare the New Testament, published in London, with the genuine Roman Catholic Bible published in Lisbon. They promised to make their findings public. In due course the following appeared in the press: 'We are now authorized to declare that there does not exist in Portuguese a new edition of any book so accurate and perfect as the 1860 edition of the New Testament translated by Antônio Pereira de Figueiredo. Signed: A Catholic-Protestant.'

Goulart was further aided in his work by the representative of the Episcopal Protestant Foreign Missionary Society in the city, the Rev. Richard Holden, a Scotsman. He proved a great help and gave him every encouragement.

Wherever the messengers of the cross were persecuted in Brazil some men, more observing and less prejudiced, rose to defend them.

Bernardino's conversion

The conversion of Bernardino G. da Silva illustrates the tactics followed by the missionary-minded members of the Fluminense Church. Bernardino lived on the sea-front in the Santa Luzia district of Rio. He was a prosperous man, owning two businesses, a butcher's shop and a general store. A customer of his had a neighbour who worked with Jardim at the dockyard and to this man Jardim preached the gospel. Each evening the man recounted to his friend all that Jardim had said during the day, and the friend for his part recounted it to Bernardino. The latter had a Bible and daily he poured over its pages to discover if the gospel was as Jardim declared it to be. News filtered back to the dockyard that there was a seeking soul in Santa Luzia, so the following Sunday Jardim walked into the store as Bernardino was selling shirts to a customer. Jardim asked him if he had a Bible and if he read it. Reluctantly, even fearfully, Bernardino confessed that he had a Bible and yes, he read it. He was expecting to be accused of a criminal offence and arrested! Instead Jardim enquired if he believed the Bible and, if so, why did he break the Sabbath by opening his shop on Sunday? Bernardino made the usual excuses: his competitors opened on Sundays; it was the day he did most business; if he closed on Sunday his customers would leave him and he would lose his means of livelihood and, he added, he had a family to support. With an impatient gesture, characteristic of the incisive witness of those early days, Jardim brushed aside the man's excuses and opened the Bible at Hebrews 13:5: 'Be free from the love of money, content with such things as ye have, for he hath said, I will never leave thee nor forsake thee. So that we may boldly say, The Lord is my helper, and I will not fear what man shall do unto me.' The conversation lasted for three hours, but at the end Bernardino had been won for Christ. The next Saturday notices were nailed to the doors of both businesses to the effect that God had ordained that man should work six days and his Sabbath must be kept; therefore the stores would not be open for business the following day. The losses during the first month or so were so heavy that Bernardino almost succumbed, but his new friends at the Fluminense Church helped him and gradually material prosperity returned. He learned a first and valuable lesson, as the Englishman Clarke had done, that the Lord is no man's debtor, but he honours those who honour him.

Bernardino began to hold meetings in his own home during the week. At first they were well attended, but in the course of a few weeks numbers dropped and interest waned. He learned a second lesson: that no man can come to the Father unless he draw him.

Believers under arrest

Persecution was inevitable. One evening nine men were seated round a table in Bernardino's kitchen studying the Bible together. In the shadows, around the walls, sat the women and children listening to the exposition of the Word of God. There was a knock at the door! A police inspector entered, followed by a posse of constables, and ordered the immediate arrest of all the men present; he would have taken the women and children too had Bernardino not pointed out that the men were the guilty ones, and the women and children should be allowed to return to their homes. The following day while the men were in custody the women were visited by the police who attempted to intimidate them into renouncing their faith. Although these women were ignorant and unlettered each in her turn answered the questions put to her with such assurance that the authorities were finally forced to desist and leave them all alone.

When the men were led off to prison they created quite a stir in the neighbourhood. Each believer was escorted by two policemen, and the whole populace turned out to see them pass down the street. In due course each was arraigned before the magistrates and closely examined as to his beliefs and manner of life.

Jardim's witness was typical of what the others also declared. He explained how they met together for worship and the study of God's Word, and so learned of God's love for sinful men and of his salvation through Christ. He quoted Scripture with such facility that the chief inquisitor confiscated the Bible, first having demanded that the passages quoted be clearly marked. Towards the end of the interview this same man felt that he could no longer trust his own hearing since the accumulated testimony was so 'other-worldly'. He closed the proceedings by declaring: 'Enough, enough! I seem to be in another world!'

The prisoners were sent to the Central Police Court and there appeared before the judge. This high dignitary, thinking that he had before him a group of ignorant men of the poorer class, harangued them on the dangers of reading a false Bible published by the British who twisted the meaning to suit their own way of thinking. He added that the true Bible was published by the Roman Catholic Church – the Figueiredo version translated directly from the Vulgate. His astonishment knew no bounds when Jardim, with quiet erudition, proved that there was no essential difference between the Protestant version and the Catholic – both were Figueiredo! Another high official, present at the hearing, scoffed that if he, as a *doutor* had difficulty in understanding the Bible, how much more difficulty would a 'bunch of ignorant peasants' have. At this Jardim opened the Bible and requested the judge to read Luke 10:21: 'In that hour Jesus rejoiced in spirit, and said, I thank thee, O Father, Lord of heaven and earth, that thou hast hid these things from the wise and prudent, and hast revealed them unto babes: even so, Father, for so it seemed good in thy sight.' The court was at a loss to know what to do, preferring not to argue any longer, so the case was dismissed and the prisoners released.

Four of them were not released, however, since the police inspector who had made the arrest was not satisfied with the court's decision. He demanded that Jardim and the others should sign a document to the effect that they would hold no more house meetings, but they preferred to stay in prison rather than sign. Pitt visited them there and returned to the church saying that they were rejoicing in their suffering for Christ's sake. They were in the middle of a prayer meeting when the order came from higher authorities for their immediate and unconditional release. Not a man rose from his knees until prayer was finished. The police confessed that they had never before handled such strange prisoners!

The ultimate result of the persecution was good – it strengthened the faith of the believers; police and criminals in the gaol heard the gospel; the authorities had learned that they were dealing with men of strong convictions and well-grounded in their faith; the publicity in the press aroused greater interest in the gospel. However, on more than one occasion attempts were made to put a stop to the meetings by mob violence.

Mob violence

In August 1861, for example, a mob, instigated by fanatical elements, gathered in the street outside the house where meetings were being held. By this time Francisco da Gama had moved to more commodious premises in order to accommodate better the growing congregation. On this occasion the doctor himself was present, as were citizens from Britain, Portugal, France, Switzerland, Spain and the U.S.A., the congregation at that time being truly international. The police appeared but made no attempt to deter the violence. Stones rained on the roof and were thrown through the windows. At one point the mob tried to storm the house. Fortunately it was built on a rock high above the road and approached by a stone stairway, so a well-aimed bottle, thrown from above, hit the wall and showered the would-be assailants with broken glass. It undoubtedly saved the believers from being severely manhandled. A police inspector appeared and silenced the mob, and then asked courteously to speak to Dr Kalley personally. The request was granted and, as a result, two policemen were left on duty at the door and the crowd dispersed. There was, however, further trouble, as the homes of believers were damaged by the mob.

Later, similar scenes were witnessed on the other side of the Bay of Guanabara, in Niteroi, where the preaching of the gospel was attracting large crowds. There, in 1864, the mob became so violent that only direct intervention by the state police, with drawn swords, prevented Dr and Mrs Kalley from being lynched. In this case one of the rioters was arrested but later released unpunished. Dr Kalley lodged a complaint with both the British and American ambassadors as also with the chief of police. He also interviewed the governor of the state personally and, as a result, a policy of severe repression of such disturbances was implemented. Order was restored and meetings were held unmolested.

These incidents were to serve as a pattern for mob violence against evangelical Protestants in later years. Fanatics, often the priests themselves, would stir up the mob to violence until pressure was put on the state to intervene. Token arrests would be made but the rioters apprehended would go unpunished. The Roman Catholic Church was the state church, but it was the policy of the state to keep the church in subordination. In official circles the Catholic Church was not popular, but it was too powerful an organization to thwart, unless for constitutional reasons. The believers would never, in any circumstances, press for the prosecution of their persecutors: they prayed for them and sought to win them for Christ, often successfully! Local authorities, too, even when wholly sympathetic with the gospel cause, avoided taking severe measures against offenders in order to prevent Catholics from awarding a martyr's halo to the one punished. It was a well-known policy for turbulent priests to court arrest in order to arouse their followers to greater frenzy – the 'faithful shepherd of the flock' behind prison bars because of the obnoxious Protestants!

17.
Labours crowned with success

Dr Kalley proved himself to be a true missionary statesman. He had invited experienced laymen to leave their newly found haven of freedom and comfort in the United States and go to Brazil to serve as the nucleus around which the Brazilian church would be built. Laymen though they were, he vested them with authority in the new church: they and their converts would meet together, under the chairmanship of their pastor – in those early days Dr Kalley himself – to decide and legislate on church matters.

The Fluminense Church and its officers

The Congregational form of church government was established, the formal meeting of church members being the decision-making assembly. The local church was independent, not subject to any superior body and its members coresponsible for the well-being of their church. Elders and deacons were appointed to serve, not as a legislative body, but as counsellors. In the church meeting they were merely voting members, alongside everyone else.

Dr Kalley was a Presbyterian by birth and upbringing but in Brazil his outlook on church polity changed: he became a practising Congregationalist. Several reasons may be adduced for this change in outlook. The doctor was an avowed 'independent'. He stoutly denied that he was a 'Presbyterian' but considered himself a Christian, a member of the church of Christ. He had been in close association with the Congregational Church in Britain: it was a Congregational minister who had sponsored his application to the London Missionary Society and that body was largely Congregational, and, not least, he had married into the Wilson-Morley families, traditionally staunch Congregational dissenters. There was, however, one overriding factor of a practical nature: the spiritual maturity and trustworthiness of the believers in the newly established Fluminense Church; local church affairs could be left safely with them. William Pitt, Francisco da Gama, Francisco de Souza Jardim were among the founding members and others, of equal calibre, came afterwards, for example, Bernardino Guilherme da Silva. One other was to play a leading role in the congregation, José Luiz Fernandes Braga. His dynamic and wholly consecrated personality was to make its influence felt in every activity of the church for some fifty years.

In October 1868 a small group of believers rowed out to a ship from Europe anchored in Guanabara Bay. There were ninety passengers on board, eighty-two of them Portuguese. The believers went to present the claims of the gospel to the newcomers to Brazil. A service was held and among the immigrants who heard the message was the young man José Luiz Fernandes Braga. He was mildly interested in what he heard, but never imagined that he, like Paul, was destined to carry that message to his own countrymen and to proclaim the Lord's name 'before kings and rulers'. He had come to Brazil with high hopes of making a fortune. Brazil offered him every opportunity of doing so, and he possessed the essential characteristics of the successful business man: intelligence, initiative, tenacity of purpose and an indomitable will. He expected to find gold in the narrow squalid streets of Rio de Janeiro, but instead he found Christ. He became friendly with a business associate, João Manoel Gonçalves dos Santos, later to serve as the first national pastor of the Fluminense Church. Both were lads of sixteen years of age. Santos had heard the gospel and had just been converted. With all the ardour of a new convert he sought to win Braga for Christ. He persuaded him to attend the Sunday meetings held in the home of the Madeiran, Francisco da Gama.

Braga was soon rejoicing in the fulness of the abundant life in Christ, and anxious to consecrate all his energies to the propagation of his newly-found faith. There was, however, a

serious obstacle: he worked in his brother's hat factory and
that included working on Sunday too. Since he was obliged to
work on Sunday that prevented him from being baptized and
becoming a member of the church. No one who was forced to
work on Sundays could be a member of the Fluminense
Church. Those early believers considered Sabbath observance to be a testimony to the gospel, and indeed it was so
since in Brazil everything continued on Sunday just as on
weekdays in industry, commerce and markets. Sunday was
the busiest day of the whole week and all employees were
obliged to work on that day to cope with the extra business.
For a Brazilian to refuse to work on Sunday as a matter of
principle was a novelty as well as a testimony. In such circumstances it was not easy for a believer to obtain work and,
when he did, it was usually of an inferior nature with little
prospect of betterment.

Young Braga was on the horns of a dilemma: if he continued to work on Sunday it would be in disobedience to the
revealed will of God, and yet if he refused to do so his brother
would dispense with his services and that would end his
dreams of material prosperity. He found his brother adamant: he would make no concessions to the scruples of his
younger brother. However, Braga did not hesitate, but
sacrificed the material for the spiritual and so set an abiding
principle for his future. He would follow the dictates of
conscience however costly such a course of action might be.
The initial step was indeed costly. Braga was out of work. He
eventually found other employment but with no material
prospects whatever. However, shortly afterwards his brother
died and Braga fell heir to the business. He took it over and
remodelled it on Christian principles – no work on Sundays,
benefits for the workers, scrupulous honesty in every trans-
action – and the firm prospered. In 1871 he married Christina
Faulhaber who, as a girl, had attended Mrs Kalley's Sunday
School class in Petropolis. She was his true help-meet, aiding
him in his all-consuming desire to extend the kingdom of
Christ.

Such were the men who helped to imbue the Fluminense
Church with a healthy spirit of nationalism and independence. The first evangelical church in Brazil was indigenous
from its inception. Founded by an independent missionary it

was nurtured in the spirit of self-reliance, under God, by these stalwarts. It was written of Dr Kalley: 'He was a great man, of a deep, penetrating understanding and of irreproachable character, a true Puritan and, as such, he attracted men and moulded them into a valiant band of helpers, equally zealous for Christ and his cause. People might deride them for their faith, but in their dealings with them were forced to acknowledge their honesty and trustworthiness.'

In the nascent Fluminense Church there were difficulties of a very practical nature. For example, an Englishman, who had been living with a Brazilian woman and had children by her, was converted and wished to marry her. The only legal marriage was that performed by a Roman Catholic priest; no provision was made for the marriage of non-Catholics. The doctor consulted the church and finally, together, they devised a form of 'marriage by contract'. The marriage ceremony was performed, documents were signed provisionally, to be legalized as soon as competent laws were passed ending the dominance of the Roman Catholic Church. The burial of the dead also constituted a difficulty as cemeteries were closed to non-Catholics.

Hymn-writing

One of the greatest contributions made by the Kalleys to the Fluminense Church, indeed, to the church as a whole in Brazil, was the hymnbook called *Salmos e Hinos* (Psalms and Hymns), which is still today the best and most popular of hymnals in the country. Both the doctor and his wife translated hymns from English or German, and they also composed hymns of their own. Dr Kalley wrote his first hymn in Madeira, in the summer of 1842, and it was followed by others, notably one composed in prison in 1843: 'Here we suffer grief and pain'. It is probable that the doctor finalized the composition of this hymn as he stood on the deck of the S.S. *William* and watched dense clouds of smoke arising from the burning of his property in Santa Luzia, as it was also from the other fire of burning Bibles kindled in the central square of the town!

As he was a Scot the doctor's translations were taken from

the Scottish Psalter, but on his marriage to Sarah, an English-woman and a Congregationalist, translations and compositions of hymns became more frequent. 'Of the two, Mrs Kalley had the greater poetic gift,' asserts the Rev. Edward Moreira in his short biography of the Kalleys. 'Dr Kalley in his compositions was always doctrinally orientated: his wife, on the other hand, adorned and illustrated doctrine with her poetic skill. The Kalleys composed the first hymns in Portuguese to stand the test of time. Their forerunners, missionaries to the Portuguese in the Far East, composed hymns that are purely of historic value. The Kalleys' hymns are still sung with enthusiasm and unction.'

The first hymnbook, published in 1861, just three years after the founding of the Fluminense Church, contained fifty hymns, eighteen metric Psalms and thirty-two hymns. It was first used by the congregation on 17 November under the title *Psalms and Hymns*, with the additional words: 'for the use of those who love our Lord Jesus Christ'. The church was now equipped for worship – it had the Scriptures and a hymnbook. Three years later a further six hymns were included in the collection.

Mrs Kalley composed new hymns constantly, some written for special occasions such as the inauguration of a new church meeting-place, a church anniversary, the reorganization of the Sunday School, etc. By 1865 the book had grown to a total of eighty-three: twenty-five metric Psalms and fifty-eight hymns. Eventually, these early editions were completed by the publication of a music book in 1868, with seventy-six different tunes. Later, successive editions of both words and music books were to be published.

Mrs Kalley taught all the hymns to the congregation and, in addition, held music classes on Monday evenings. In her preface to the music edition she reminds the hymn-singers 'not to shout, nor yet to drag the hymns, but to pay particular attention to the words being sung rather than the music and to sing them to the praise of the great Saviour to whom we must consecrate the best of our faculties and abilities in lives so blessed by him'.

Presbyterian missionaries in Rio

Four years after Dr Kalley founded the church in Rio de Janeiro, the first missionary of the Presbyterian Board of Foreign Mission, the Rev. Ashbel Green Simonton, arrived. The date was 12 August 1859. He was the forerunner of American missions in Brazil. A year later he would be joined by his brother-in-law Rev. A.L. Blackford.

Immediately on arrival Rev. Simonton visited Dr Kalley and marvelled at all that the doctor had accomplished alone and without the aid of a missionary society. Difficulties arose between them. The doctor committed a grave error – he wrote an open letter, unsigned, and had it delivered to Rev. Simonton in a circuitous manner through no less than four messengers. In an oblique way he levelled unjust criticism at the Presbyterians for beginning work in the Rio area where the Fluminense Church was already well established, when the whole of vast Brazil still awaited the gospel. He declared he had 'made a small clearing' in a vast forest and was cultivating it: was it right for someone to invade that 'clearing' and settle there, intending to cultivate it too? Rev. Simonton was highly offended, more at the way the note had been written and made public than about its contents. He recognized that the doctor had a right to his opinions, so he acted promptly and in a correct manner. He asked the doctor to meet him and presented him with a reasoned and courteous explanation of his position as to why he considered the criticism to be unfounded and offensive. He then demanded an apology. The doctor asked for time to consider the matter and after two hours they met again. The doctor then presented a full apology which was graciously accepted. The two men knelt down and prayed, shook hands and considered the matter closed. Rev. Simonton then spoke freely of his plans for the future and won the approval of his older colleague.

The doctor did make amends. He wrote to each of the messengers and requested them to forget the note was ever written. The two men remained firm friends until Rev. Simonton's early and untimely death. At one time Rev. Simonton overstretched himself and needed rest. He went to Petropolis and, after staying first in a hotel, accepted the Kalleys' insistent invitation to be their guest. He wrote, 'Every afternoon

I attended worship at Dr Kalley's home. It was a great privilege to take part in worship so simple and evangelical such as he takes. He appears to be above all a man of faith. What impressed me was his evident consciousness of the presence of the great and holy God, and his communion with him. He expounds the simple truth and yet it is evident that his thoughts range wide and deep.'

Rev. Simonton gave full credit to Dr Kalley for the able manner in which he had prepared the ground-work for missions; the right for the Protestant to propagate his faith had been established constitutionally; the position of the foreign missionary was legally secure; the Brazilian Protestant community had legal status; a hymnal had already been prepared; lastly, and probably the greatest contribution of all, a trained and experienced body of colporteurs was at work and poised for an ever-expanding ministry. Years later, another Presbyterian missionary, Dr Lane, wrote, 'The work of the colporteur is the right arm of the missionary: that which he does in the distribution of the Word cannot be underestimated: his maintenance is an indispensable condition for the continuance of the work.' To these five basics a sixth would be added later: the interpretation of relevant articles of the constitution.

In 1863, Rev. Blackford moved from Rio de Janeiro to São Paulo and began work in that city. His first meetings were held in the home of William Pitt, Dr Kalley's first helper and a member of the Fluminense Church. Incidentally, he introduced the *paulistas* to a novelty, paraffin!

Mr Pitt was already a seasoned, experienced soul-winner. Possibly his greatest convert was William Esher, an Irishman and the progenitor of a famous Presbyterian family in Brazil. Mr Pitt was eventually ordained as a Presbyterian minister, but his ministry was short-lived. He died shortly after his ordination. Rev. Simonton, too, died. His ministry also was short but very effective: he and Rev. Blackford between them had established the Presbyterian cause in Brazil.

Correspondence and literary achievements

Dr Kalley was a prodigious writer: his busy pen rarely rested.

He wrote all his sermons and, in doing so, revealed his orderly mind, his profound grasp of biblical truth and his facility in communication. He could convey the deepest spiritual truths in simple language, easily understood by his hearers, even though many of them neither knew how to read or write. Some of his sermons merit publication and are as relevant today as when they were delivered.

He maintained a steady stream of correspondence with people in Britain, the U.S.A., the West Indies, Portugal and Madeira, and the letters he wrote were not a chatty retailing of family news, but were weighty with scriptural answers to church problems. His Bible knowledge and his vast experience were freely at the disposal of those who consulted him. The question of baptism by immersion, as opposed to aspersion, had caused havoc in the Illinois churches; a colporteur, member of the Fluminense Church, was languishing in jail in Portugal; John Morley, his wife's relative, was in doubt and confusion as a result of the teaching of J.N. Darby; in Lisbon lack of firm leadership and a teaching ministry was creating problems; his personal investments in American railways were causing his financial advisor in London concern. All these matters and many more came to rest on the doctor's desk. He had no secretary but attended to each letter personally.

He was a great opportunist. The daily press provided him with material for articles to be published in the papers, principally in the *Correio Mercantil* (the 'Commercial Telegraph'). The following titles are an indication of the variety of subjects dealt with: 'The Rule of our Faith', 'An Important Confession', 'Jesuitism in Parliament', 'What is the World?', '*Imperium Brasilense* and *Imperio Eclesiastico*', 'The Holy Scriptures', 'The Penalty of Excommunication'. He used a pseudonym, 'The Critic', or sometimes, 'The Catholic-Protestant', and wrote a total of thirty-five articles for the *Telegraph* alone! Then, too, he wrote letters to the press, usually to correct a misinterpretation, malicious or otherwise, of Protestant belief and practice.

Religious freedom was dear to his heart and it is interesting to note that defenders of such freedom, politicians, often used the doctor's reasoned arguments when opposing the intolerance of the Roman Catholic Church in Parliament.

The Kalleys also translated Bunyan's works *The Holy War* and *Pilgrim's Progress*, and published them first in the daily press in serial form and then, at the request of readers, in book form. Later, Mrs Kalley wrote John Bunyan's biography and had it published. The doctor, for his part, compiled a few devotional books: *Cleon and Maia, The Happiness of the Home* and *Short Prayers*.

One publication of the doctor's, however, caused a considerable stir, *The Thief on the Cross*. The book had been printed in Britain but was impounded by Customs in Rio de Janeiro because of the illustration on the cover. There was a law on the statute books which prohibited the publication of anything against the religion of the state, and the customs officials held that the illustration contravened that law. When pressed for an explanation, since such scenes of the crucifixion were commonplace in churches throughout the land, the officials said that the church believed that the thieves were not nailed to the cross, as indicated on the cover of the book, but tied there with ropes! It took intervention at the highest level to get the books released and, diplomatically, the doctor changed the cover before offering the book for sale to the public through the colporteurs. Booksellers did not stock Protestant books.

Although Dr Kalley was opposed to the intolerance of the Catholic Church in Brazil, he was on friendly terms with a number of individual Roman Catholics. One of these, Dr José Luiz Malafaia, corrected the Portuguese versions of the Kalley hymns and indeed of all their publications. He was a frequent guest at their table and they attended his wedding in a Catholic Church. It was the system the doctor opposed, not the people themselves.

18.
A new helper and a new home

In 1862 Dr Kalley's ministry was again seriously interrupted, this time by an accident. He was accustomed to making long distant visits in the Petropolis area by horseback. At full gallop, on this occasion, he was thrown by his horse and sustained injuries to his leg and knee. As a result he was obliged to use crutches. Healing came slowly, almost imperceptibly, so much so that his doctor strongly recommended his return to Britain for treatment. He was very reluctant to accept this advice but was finally persuaded by his wife that such a journey would bring a threefold benefit: his injured leg would receive the best treatment possible and, it was to be hoped, be fully restored; it would give them an opportunity to seek out a helper for pastoral duties in Rio; and finally, it would make feasible a long-felt desire to revisit Palestine. So in August they embarked. There was great consternation in the church as the members feared that they would not see their pastor again!

Once in England, doctors recommended hydropathic treatment at various spas both in England and Scotland. The leg healed, the crutches were discarded, and the doctor returned to normal health and vitality. The Kalleys then made a leisurely tour of the Continent, visiting Germany, France and Switzerland, but did not proceed to Palestine as they had hoped. As opportunity offered they visited various training centres for pastors and missionaries, and in Basle thought they had found what they were looking for – a German student suited in every way to become their helper in the Fluminense Church. After due consideration, though, he declined to accept their invitation.

During their absence from Brazil correspondence flowed

freely between pastor and flock. In this way the church in Rio was able to enlarge on its problems, and the absent pastor able to exhort, encourage and nurture the believers. It was evident that the Kalleys must return to Brazil without further delay. *En route* they called at Lisbon and there met Portuguese colporteurs, members of the Fluminense Church, who were seeking at great sacrifice and with much suffering to disseminate the Word among their relatives and fellow countrymen. The visit of the Kalleys brought these men encouragement and renewed vigour.

The ship called at Madeira, and, as on their outward journey to Brazil, the Kalleys again took the opportunity of going ashore and spending the day with his sister, Jane, and her husband, Dr Miller.

Mr Holden

Dr Kalley did eventually find what he most desired – an experienced and dedicated helper, Richard Holden. He discovered him where he least expected to find him – in Brazil! In one of the doctor's letters he describes how it all came about: 'In 1862, being most unwell, I was obliged to journey to Europe. Seven months later, having sufficiently recovered – I no longer needed to use crutches – I journeyed throughout Britain in an endeavour to find someone, a true servant of the Lord, who would help me in my pastoral labours in Rio. I was unsuccessful... In September 1863, returning to Brazil empty-handed, the boat called in at Bahia, Salvador, and Mr Holden came aboard. We had a lengthy conversation, after which my wife and I continued our journey to Rio. Mr Holden then came south to Petropolis and stayed in our home for three months. We had ample opportunity to converse, especially about the church in Rio. The Rev. Holden had severed his connection with the Episcopal Missionary Society under whose auspices he had been working in Bahia. He had done so because he did not find sufficient liberty to teach and act as he felt God would have him do. He left the Episcopal Church altogether in order to be able to work freely with no restrictions. He returned to England with a recommendation from me that he contact the British and Foreign Bible Society in London. He did so and returned to Brazil to serve as the Bible Society agent in the Empire of Brazil, and to help me in my pastoral duties...'

Richard Holden was a Scot, a native of Fife, and by upbringing an Episcopalian. He had spent some time in Brazil in business and while there had learnt to speak Portuguese fluently. He felt the call to the ministry and after training in the States he had returned to Brazil under the auspices of the Episcopalian Missionary Society. He proved to be a valuable helper, a man greatly beloved by the Brazilians.

Protestant marriages and burials authorized

On his arrival back in Rio, Dr Kalley heard that the government in Brazil had decreed by law that Protestant ministers should be authorized to conduct marriage ceremonies for non-Catholics, and also to register both births and deaths. This was the outcome of a long struggle that had taken years and in which Dr Kalley was indirectly involved. The Roman Catholic Church no longer had the exclusive right to marry – now Protestant ministers also had this right. There was only one stipulation, namely, that the minister be duly elected by the local church. So in October 1863 the church met in session and formally decided that the name of the church should be the *Igreja Evangélica Fluminense* and that Dr Kalley be elected pastor. He had in fact been pastor since its inception seven years earlier, but now his position was legalized. A few days later the imperial government issued the certificate giving Dr Kalley rights which hitherto had been exclusive to the Roman clergy. All marriages by 'contract' celebrated up to that point were duly registered and made legal. A week or two later Francisco Jardim, who had lost his wife during the absence of the Kalleys in Europe, remarried and so became the first to benefit by the new law.

In the same decree provision was also made for a portion of each cemetery to be set aside for Protestant and non-Catholic burials. Up to that time Brazilians who died non-Catholics were buried in unconsecrated ground reserved for criminals and suicides. Dr Kalley's method of securing the legal rights of believers, that of stimulating the interpretation of the constitution and of promoting the passage of liberating bills in Parliament, was proving to be effective. This was his sixth contribution to the early Brazilian church.

The move to Rio

Immediately on their return to Rio the Kalleys insisted on occupying the house next door to that in which the Gamas lived and in which the congregation met for worship. It was unsuitable for a permanent residence; indeed there was urgent need not only for finding a house for themselves in the city, but also much more spacious accommodation for the growing congregation. They inspected various properties in the neighbourhood, including a street where some of the wealthy slave-traders lived. These traders used three-storied houses, the upper floors for residence and the ground floor for a 'deposit' where their 'living chattels' were kept ready, pending sale to customers. The Kalleys were unsuccessful in their search and eventually were obliged to return to Petropolis once more.

By 1864 they had accomplished much. The Fluminense Church was firmly rooted in Brazilian soil; it was registered with the authorities for the celebration of births, deaths and marriages; it had, in 1863, duly elected Dr Kalley as pastor and the Rev. Richard Holden as co-pastor. Over the Bay in Niteroi the gospel was taking hold although believers continued to suffer persecution and every form of harassment. Dr Kalley was giving increasing pastoral oversight to that struggling congregation. He and his wife did so at considerable risk. They were stoned by the rabble on various occasions and once, at least, narrowly escaped being lynched.

The colporteurs were ranging far and wide. Ten members of the church were employed selling the Scriptures, not only in the Rio area but penetrating well into the interior – to the states of Minas Gerais and Bahia. Two others were in Portugal, one in Madeira and one witnessing in Africa. The press continued to give Dr Kalley and Rev. Holden opportunities to clarify gospel issues, matters very imperfectly understood by most people and much maligned by gratuitous enemies.

A change of residence from Petropolis to Rio de Janeiro became even more imperative. For almost ten years the Kalleys had sought to live in the amenable climate of the town high in the Organ Mountains and so avoid the steaming heat of the capital city. The journey home over the Fluminense marshes by train, and then up the mountain by coach was time-consuming and exhausting and that journey they were obliged to make frequently.

Then, too, they were under great strain owing to the tempo of the persecutions in Niteroi and the reluctance of the competent authorities to take action. It was a time when Dr Kalley personally interviewed the state governor, the chief of police, the ambassadors of both Britain and the States in order to get redress for his harassed flock. If Dr and Mrs Kalley were to move to Rio then it would have to be in the vicinity of the church. They finally found a suitable property in the district of Saúde, in the Travessa das Partilhas, one of the poorer parts of old colonial Rio. A house at street level provided ample accommodation for the church and, at the back up a steep incline, known as the 'Ladeira do Barroso, no Morro do Livramento', an excellent site on which to build for themselves a house sufficiently large to meet their needs, with facilities for servants, guests and the occasional dinner party. The district of Saúde was where a number of British craftsmen lived who were employed at the naval dockyards and this was an additional factor in favour of the location. It was the area where Pitt had had a school for the children of dockyard workers.

In August 1864 the church met for the last time in the Rua do Proposito, a location which had served them for four years, and moved to their third place of worship on Dr Kalley's newly-acquired property, premises they were to occupy for the next twenty-two years. By November of that year the Kalley residence was ready for occupation. After long years the ideal was realized: church and manse were together.

19.
Dealing with problems

Disagreements with the Presbyterians

Relationships between the Presbyterians and the Fluminense Church were strained at this time. The Presbyterians, with their American background, were much less strict than Dr Kalley, who remained true to the strict discipline of Scottish sabbatarianism. The Americans were more relaxed in their approach to the norm of Christian behaviour, especially about such things as smoking, social drinking and belonging to the Masons. Trouble also arose regarding the communion service. Dr Kalley adhered to the Scottish tradition of 'fencing the Table' – that is, only allowing those who were proven Christians to participate in the taking of the bread and wine. A member of the Presbyterian Church, a Brazilian, was refused the right to take the elements when visiting the Fluminense Church on a Communion Sunday. The Presbyterians registered their protest, but the Fluminense Church reserved its right to accept or exclude communicants.

The Presbyterian missionaries also critized Dr Kalley not only for his church polity (whereas he had once been a Presbyterian he was now a thorough-going Congregational) but also over his method of missionary outreach. They thought him too 'timid' and held that there should be more publicity, a more open and public approach to the preaching of the gospel, even to the point of confrontation. The doctor insisted that too much publicity was unwise, as he had found to his cost in Madeira. There, the ecclesiastical authorities had successfully closed down his varied activities on the island: first, his medical work, then his schools and, finally, his preaching.

He preferred his own method, the dissemination of the Scriptures in an unobtrusive manner through colportage and preaching in homes and meeting halls. Even then, persecution resulted, but not through any virulent attacks on the state religion on his part. His advice to others was: 'Forget that the person to whom you are speaking is a Roman Catholic who must be made to understand that mass, confession, purgatory, the pope, are all wrong – an intellectual apprehension of this will never lead to that person's salvation – and deal with him as a sinner needing that salvation which only Christ can give him through his sacrifice. He will then be taught of God and made ready for the "House of Glory".'

In an endeavour to clarify his position the doctor sought and obtained an interview with the editor of the *Apostolo*, a Roman Catholic paper which was most virulent in attacking him. Far from this interview improving matters, the leading articles in the paper became more scathing than ever. Through the columns of the daily press, the doctor continued to defend his points of view, basing them, as was his custom, solely on the Bible.

The doctor was by no means 'timid', but as a canny Scot and a mature experienced missionary, he practised and advocated caution. Harassment might come to him, but it would come uninvited: he would not deliberately provoke it.

Slavery

No one could live in Rio, not even the Kalleys, without being fully aware of slavery – the traffic in human beings. The majority of the population in the city were slaves. At the height of the slave trade twenty to thirty thousand slaves a year were imported and sold in the Rio market. The other great slave market was in Salvador, Bahia.

The intrepid Portuguese mariners, sent by Prince Henry the Navigator to explore the west coast of Africa, had brought the first batch of slaves back to Portugal. Zurrara, the chronicler of the fifteenth century, describes in vivid language their arrival in the Algarve and the harrowing scenes when they were distributed among the prince's favourites – wives parted from their husbands, children torn from their mothers, families divided piecemeal; the sobbing, the wailing, the anguish – and the prince sitting on his charger unconcerned, comforting himself with the thought that although he was forced to enslave their bodies he had saved their souls from eternal perdition, since they would all be baptized and brought up as 'Christians'! On that infamous day, 8 August 1444, the Portuguese slave trade began, and Brazil became its most fruitful market.

After Britain freed the slaves in her colonies, principally the West Indies, she put pressure on her ally Portugal to do the same. In 1831 a law was passed in the Brazilian parliament prohibiting the importation of slaves, although the traffic continued illegally. The British navy patrolled the seas and intercepted any ship carrying slaves; the human cargo was put under the British flag and declared freed. In 1871 the law of *Ventre Livre* – free birth – would be passed. In future children born of slaves would be born free. And, finally, in 1888 the emperor's daughter, Princess Isabel, would sign the decree freeing all slaves in the empire. This, however, was still in the future at the point we have reached in our story.

In Dr Kalley's time, slaves were an indication of a person's wealth and status. When the family walked abroad in the streets, the slaves followed in 'crocodile'. Male slaves were allowed to wear only a loincloth and made to walk barefoot, unless, of course, they were coachmen or postillions. Female slaves wore a simple dress, unless they happened to be favourites with their mistress, in which case they were pampered. On the streets, slaves were much in evidence, apparently walking free. The reason for this was that in a town house of modest proportions not many slaves could be employed directly. The surplus were turned loose on the streets each morning to earn a little money selling fruit or drink, or engaging in heavy labour. At night each slave had to hand over to the master a fixed levy, the slave being allowed to keep any excess. In this way a successful slave could save enough to buy his or her freedom. There was, too, the constant transit of slaves going about their enforced duties – carrying water from the public 'fountains', dealing with stinking sewerage, bearing loads, carrying sedan chairs, working as coachmen – an endless multiplicity of tasks, and all done under the ever-present threat of the lash. Newly arrived foreigners were always horrified at the cruel treatment meted out to slaves, but usually they came to accept it as a way of life. The most moving of all scenes was that of a column of slaves under punishment, chained together with iron collars around their necks, and the chains encased in cloth so that they would not clank. The overseer walked beside them with his whip at the ready. Such scenes were witnessed by all residents in Rio, the Kalleys included, as they moved around the city. A contemporary wrote, 'Slaves fled and slaves died; against those who fled notices appeared in the daily press, and as to those who died, there existed a society which sought to stem the high rate of mortality amongst slaves – these horrors of slavery.'

Soon after his arrival in Brazil the doctor, with his penchant for writing, had expressed the desire to begin some kind of African news-sheet, specially for the slave population, but the wish never came to fruition, possibly because he realized that few slaves knew how to read. However, there is repeated mention of 'black people' gathering together to hear him talk about the gospel.

Among the growing number of members in the Fluminense Church there must have been a fair number of African slave origin. As to slaves themselves, it would not have been easy for them to attend meetings as the consent of their owners would be necessary. In the church records only the names of candidates for baptism are given with no indication of their colour or status. The question, however, did come up in 1865. A candidate for church membership, Bernardino de Oliveira Rameiro, a man who had worked with Pitt in the dockyard, was a slave-owner. At a church meeting the question was hotly debated: 'Can a believer in the Lord Jesus Christ own slaves?' At the following meetings Dr Kalley, who had the custom of giving a lengthy exhortation on a relevant topic at such a meeting, spoke on the subject: 'How should a true believer treat his slaves? What is the will of Jesus respecting this?' In a truly masterly exhortation, he pointed out that there are three ways of serving: out of love, as a son with a father; to earn money, e.g. servants, workers, etc.; by compulsion, without love, without contracts or adjustment of salaries, as a slave obliged to do what his master orders under threats, blows and torture, so without the slightest recompense. He then took the three Greek words that are used in the New Testament for 'service', translated 'deacon', 'mercenary', 'slave', and cited Paul's exhortation in Colossians 4:1: 'Masters, render to your slaves that which is just and equal, knowing that you also have a Master in heaven,' and Ephesians 6:9: '...forbear threatening ...'. He then demonstrated that there are things which belong to each person, (for example, his body with its members and functions) which cannot be handed over to another, and each has the right to make use of the body which is his in a just and honest manner for personal benefit. For a man to exercise jurisdiction over another so that nothing he possesses is his own is to be a thief and villain. 'Each one must give account of his actions to the Great Judge, when he makes his fellow-man to work for him against his will, without wages, under threat of punishment and with constant suffering, and all in order to gain substantial profits. This is violent theft of the gifts that the Creator has given to the poor creature, who in no way differs from the one who bought him.'

He then addressed the slave-owner directly: 'To you the slave is your neighbour, and comes under the great command: "Thou shalt love thy neighbour as thyself." Would you like another to treat you as a slave? The commerce of animals is lawful ... but even they must be treated humanely. The slave is not the son of his owner, nor does he serve him out of love or pleasure; he works like an animal, without receiving any recompense for his labour; he only works because he fears the threat of blows and even severe inhumane treatment on the part of the one who has robbed him of his freedom. You who do this are an enemy of the Christ and cannot be a member of the church of Christ, of the Jesus who redeemed us from the curse and gave us freedom and made us children of God (Romans 8:15,16).'

The outcome of the debate is not registered but it is clear that the pastor judged the slave-owner unworthy of church membership, and with this ruling the church would be in full agreement.

Gathering clouds

By this time the co-pastor, the Rev. Richard Holden, was demonstrating his true worth. Under his guidance the Bible Society improved in efficiency, and in the Fluminense Church he relieved Dr Kally of many onerous duties. The Brazilians would describe him with a single word: *simpático* – one who is open-hearted, easily approached, kindly disposed, generous to a fault and filled with compassion. All this Richard Holden was – a true and tried friend to the Kalleys and a dedicated shepherd of souls to the church. Brazilians loved him, but their affection in no way diminished their love and veneration for Dr Kalley and his wife, 'Dona Sarah'. It was a felicitous arrangement and a greatly blessed ministry. There were, however, clouds gathering on the horizon: Dr Kalley's poor health, and the influence on Richard Holden of the teachings of John Nelson Darby, founder of the Plymouth Brethren movement.

Then, too, early in December 1866 Mrs Kalley heard of her father's sudden death a month earlier. The news was devastating since she, the eldest daughter, and her father had been very close, and he had always taken a lively interest in her work among the Portuguese-speaking people. From Sherwood Hall in Nottinghamshire, his home for the previous ten years, he had given the Kalleys every encouragement in their work. His loss was not only a severe personal blow but also a loss to the work.

20.
A well-earned break

In spite of frequent visits to towns in the Organ Mountains –
Petropolis, Teresopolis, Novo Friburgo – with their more
bracing climate, Dr Kalley's health continued to deteriorate.
Whenever he returned home to Rio he found the climate
there so excessively hot and moist that he was drained physically. He suffered from frequent attacks of migraine, and yet
he never allowed his physical condition to interfere with his
missionary activities. He applied himself to the task of
making the gospel known with unabated zeal.

Then came a crisis – a heart attack. He was down town,
returning from a visit to Niteroi, when the first attack of intensive pain crippled him. He managed to stagger home, with
frequent rests to relieve his breathing. Being a doctor he easily diagnosed his trouble, a diagnosis confirmed by his own
physician, Dr Fairburn, an Englishman practising in Rio. He
was ordered to take complete rest – no preaching, no letter-
writing, no administrative worries – and strongly recommended a return to Britain for further treatment. Mrs Kalley,
who had for a long time been advocating a prolonged fur-
lough, insisted that the time had come to take one. It was with
great reluctance that the doctor prepared to leave, possibly
for good, his home on the Ladeira do Barroso, the church and
Brazil.

The members of the church were desolated and showed
their emotion openly as only Portuguese and Brazilians can.
Amid scenes of uncontrolled emotion Dr Kalley preached his
final sermon, based on Acts 20: 17-38, and took a sorrowful
leave of the church. The man who had led these people to
Christ, nurtured them and provided for them was their good

shepherd. On 2 December 1868, the Kalleys embarked in Rio on a paddle steamer, *Panamá,* and began their long journey across the Atlantic. They made good use of their short stay in Lisbon, visiting Fluminense believers and others who lived and laboured there. After a month's sailing they reached Liverpool and were warmly welcomed by the Morleys and other relatives and friends.

As to the doctor's condition, expert medical opinion was unanimous that in all probability he would make a complete recovery, but absolute rest was prescribed, a thing he found very frustrating. Correspondence shows that the Kalleys moved around the country to Mansfield, Woburn, Pitlochry and Rothesay. As recovery was established and better health returned Dr Kalley began to engage once more in extensive letter-writing. He wrote long pastoral letters to the flock in Rio. He feared that 'ravening wolves' would enter the church and he insisted that the best way to meet such a threat was a thorough knowledge of the Bible coupled with mature Christian experience. At the same time he requested and received detailed accounts of the work in Portugal. Neither did he forget the believers in Illinois. One of his friends called him 'a warm-hearted, brave strong spirit with a busy mind and pen'.

More direct news reached him of the church in Rio with the arrival of Miss Marianne Pitt, Mrs Kalley's faithful companion. She had stayed on at the house in Rio but now, at the Kalleys' request, had joined them in Rothesay. She was a very active member of the Fluminense Church and brought welcome news of progress there.

Return to Palestine

With the return of health and vigour, Dr Kalley resolved to fulfil a long-felt desire to revisit the Holy land. His medical advisers were insistent that he should not spend the winter in Scotland, and what better climate could there be than that of Palestine? They embarked at Leith, accompanied by Marianne, their first destination being Hamburg. From there they made their way south through Germany and on to Switzerland, visiting *en route* places of historic 'spiritual' interest, such as Prague, associated with John Huss. They went on to

Italy, and reached Florence, a city they particularly wanted to visit, not only because of its art treasures but also because it was the place where Savanarola was martyred. There they met an old friend of Dr Kalley's from Malta days, Dr Luigi de Sanctis, a converted Roman Catholic priest and a well-known intellectual. The story of his conversion is unique. He was commissioned by the Vatican to prepare a series of popular lectures on the errors of the heretics, the Protestants, and in defence of the Holy Mother Roman Catholic Church. At that time Protestantism was making serious inroads into Italy. Dr Luigi asked permission to study Protestant literature as a necessary preparation for this monumental task, as he then considered it to be, but the more he studied the more convinced he became of the inherent weakness of Roman Catholic dogmas, and the strength of the biblical gospel. He was converted and, like Paul before him, he now fervently preached the faith he had formerly persecuted. The Kalleys and the Luigis spent days together in Florence enjoying one another's company, then, on the eve of the Kalleys' departure to continue their journey, they received news of Dr Luigi's sudden death. Shocked at the loss of so close a friend they delayed their journey until after the funeral.

Their itinerary took them to Corfu and on to Smyrna, to the amphitheatre where Polycarp was martyred. They sailed by Patmos, Rhodes and Cyprus on a boat which collected some 200 pilgrims going to Mecca. Dr Kalley's one regret was that his Arabic was not sufficient to converse with them about the Bible and Christ! After some ten weeks of sailing they disembarked at Beirut, a place which for both held memories of momentous happenings twenty years previously. They paid a visit to Damascus and the Baalbec ruins. Dr Kalley suffered an accident there which fortunately did not have serious consequences: he was kicked by a horse.

In Beirut they renewed their acquaintance with Dr W.M. Thomson, a missionary in Syria and Palestine, and under his guidance they planned their trip through the Holy Land. At that time, trips of that nature, if they were to be accomplished in comfort and with relative safety, needed careful preparation. Good saddle horses, pack animals, camping equipment, including tents, had to be bought and, not least, the services of a good 'dragoman' had to be arranged. All this entailed considerable expenditure and time-consuming attention to detail.

They travelled south through Sidon and Tyre and on to Galilee, camping each night and resting during the scorching heat of the day. Progress was slow, but they were now following in the steps of the Master and there was much to see and to absorb. Nazareth thrilled them since they found there a well-established missionary work, and had the good fortune to hear a sermon preached by a famous Congregational minister from Britain. Sites and scenes prominent in the New Testament were visited – the Sea of Galilee, the Mount of the Beatitudes, Capernaum, Corazim. With New Testament in hand they drank in all the atmosphere and history of such sacred territory. While in the area they took the opportunity of going to Safed, where the doctor had spent several months on a former visit, but sadly they could find no one who could recall his stay amongst them. They journeyed on south through Samaria and Bethlehem and, finally, to Jerusalem. Their first impression of the city was one of shock, since so much of it was in ruins, and everywhere seemed so dirty and neglected. As their stay became more prolonged they discovered that it had such an aura as they had never experienced in any other place; to them it became the Holy City. It was explored, savoured and enjoyed. All the time, indeed throughout the whole journey, Dr Kalley was taking photographs and preparing for illustrated talks that he would give with such telling effect later.

They then moved on to Egypt and the Pyramids, Cairo and Alexandria, returning home via Marseilles and France. It was while they were in France that news reached them of William Pitt's death. Marianne mourned the loss of a brother, and the Kalleys the loss of one of their most valued helpers. By now, Dr Kalley was fully recovered, as the exhausting tour through Europe and the Middle East had proved, and they could plan their return to Brazil.

Good news from Brazil

In the meantime what had been happening in Brazil? The Fluminense Church had discovered in the Rev. Holden a true pastor who continued to instruct them and exhort them to holy living. Correspondence had flowed freely between the Kalleys and Mr Holden, as indeed to other members of the Rio church. These letters from Brazil contained detailed accounts of conversions and baptisms, and the Rev. Holden recounted the story of the conversion of one particular young man, Dias Barros. It was typical of what was happening all the time in Rio. The young man was employed as a cashier. He was a staunch Catholic and bitterly opposed to the *Bíblias*, as the Protestants were called. Nine years before he had purchased a Bible from Gama, the colporteur. For reasons that he could not explain he began to read the Bible and discovered, to his consternation, that his brand of Catholicism was diametrically opposed to what he was reading in the Bible. He destroyed his icons and images and then discovered something more in the Bible: 'He that does not carry his cross cannot be my disciple.' He informed his boss that he would no longer work on Sunday. On occasion he had noticed a man passing along the street with a book under his arm that looked like a Bible. He accosted the man, who gladly took him to a service in the Fluminense Church. Barros lost his job but found his Saviour and began to preach the faith he had so violently opposed. As well as baptisms the Rev. Holden celebrated seven marriage ceremonies in 1868, and details were related to Dr Kalley.

Influence of the Plymouth Brethren

After Dr Kalley's return from Palestine, while staying in Crieff, he maintained a discussion by correspondence with Mr Darby. The doctor could not agree with Mr Darby's points of view regarding the church and its ministry, especially the calling and maintaining of a pastor. He also disagreed with Mr Darby's deviations on justification and sanctification. His difficulty was further compounded by the fact that his wife's uncle, Mr Morley, was adopting Darby's doctrines and was in the process of becoming a Plymouth Brother!

The Fluminense Church now numbered 150 members, and since the Kalleys' return to Britain every letter expressed the intense desire on the part of the church to have the doctor and his wife back in their midst. 'They want Robert', wrote Mrs Kalley in her diary. There was a menacing cloud on the horizon. Reading between the lines of the numerous letters that Mr Holden sent to the doctor, it appeared that he did not anticipate staying much longer as co-pastor of the Fluminense Church. Like so many good men of his day he was greatly influenced by the particular doctrines of the Plymouth Brethren, and felt that he could no longer serve as a pastor in the accepted sense of the term and receive a pastoral allowance from the church. If Mr Holden persisted in his plan then the doctor would have to find another helper. He searched for a suitable candidate in the homeland but was unsuccessful. His mind then turned to a young man in the Fluminense Church who some years previously had felt the call to the ministry, João Manoel Gonçalves dos Santos. For years Santos had served as secretary of the church and had shown admirable qualities as an administrator. He was a good preacher too, and a man of mature and irreproachable character. He had been unable to follow through his call owing to the fact that he had been nominated 'tutor' to his younger sister. He and his sister had been left orphans and Brazilian law required that until the girl became of age or married she should be under the tutelage of one legally appointed for that purpose. The sister was now married and her brother freed, therefore, from the responsibility of caring for her. The doctor knew that the young man would require special training and with this in view he appealed to his friend, Spurgeon, whose Pastors' College was now well established. Spurgeon readily offered his help to train a young Brazilian for the ministry.

Journey back to Brazil

The journey back to Brazil now began in earnest. The Kalleys took leave of his friends and relatives in Glasgow, and of her brothers and family in Sheffield. Then before embarking on 29 April 1871 they stayed with the Morleys in Upper Clapton. *En route* for Brazil they spent a month in Portugal. They had been there on three previous occasions and the Portuguese believers, some of them members of the Fluminense Church, had greatly appreciated the doctor's teaching ministry. Between visits contact had been maintained with the believers by correspondence, letters of instruction, exhortation and comfort. In Lisbon Dr Kalley met with the leaders of the various groups of believers in the city and it was there, too, that he gave his first illustrated lecture on Palestine, and especially on Jerusalem. About a hundred people listened with rapt attention and they also heard, interspersed with the lecture, the gospel message. The Kalleys also visited Porto in the north, breaking their journey at Coimbra, noted for its uni-versity. In Porto they ministered to both the British and the Portuguese. There has always been a strong British presence in Porto owing to the wine trade, much of which was in British hands. Dr Kalley gave another lecture on Palestine and at the same time preached the gospel. He proved to be a great help to the Rev. Moreton, pioneer of the British Methodist mission-ary work in the country. Back in Lisbon the Kalleys busied themselves writing letters, taking meetings, enjoying the fellowship of believers and taking steps to see that the Bible Society supplied the colporteurs with the literature they needed. Right up to the time of their sailing they were well occupied. On the last Sunday, 4 June, the doctor spoke at a meeting in the afternoon and at 6 o'clock the boat left for Brazil! Fifteen days later the ship cast anchor in the Bay of Guanabara. The Kalleys were back in Brazil once more.

21.
Renewed activity in Rio

It was Sunday, and the Fluminense Church awaited expectantly the arrival of the pastor and his wife at the Travessa das Partilhas. When they finally arrived, after all the hassle of disembarkation, what scenes of radiant joy – the Brazilian *abraço*, tears of gratitude, exclamations of praise to God! Mrs Kalley wrote, 'The noise and confusion of our disembarking were intolerable: so much baggage and so many people crowding into Customs. We finally reached the meeting house,' and then she adds in a characteristic understatement, 'The people received us with a most moving manifestation of love which comforted our hearts.'

The Kalleys soon picked up the threads of routine life once more. Little had changed in Rio itself. Modes of transport had been updated; the old omnibuses had gone and were replaced by *bondes,* trams drawn on rails by mules – one mule for short distances, and two for the suburbs. There was also a new railway line going south in the direction of São Paulo. Some of the streets were cobbled and better illuminated at night.

A new phase in the history of the church in Brazil was beginning: the American Presbyterians were now well established in Rio and São Paulo, in the latter, both in the city and in the state; Baptists, Methodists and Episcopalians would soon follow, all with their differing forms of baptism, church government and discipline. The country was vast, but the work established by these various denominations overlapped. Dissensions and difficulties were inevitable, although the difficulties were of a secondary nature since all preached exactly the same gospel, but these differences tended to loom large in inter-church relationships.

New developments in the Fluminense Church

At the end of June Mr Holden embarked for England, uncertain as to whether he would return to Brazil, or what his future plans would be. After the gruelling time he had had in Rio de Janeiro, the rest and change of his native village in Fife would afford him leisure to reassess his position. The church had learned to esteem him for his works' sake, and fervently hoped and prayed that he would come back again.

Certain changes in the church were urgent, not least the total reorganization of the Sunday School. Up to this time it had been a chaotic mixture of young and old, little or no distinction being made between the needs of one group or the other. The church resolved that there must be a clearly marked division of age groups into separate classes, with more competent teachers and more systematic teaching. Sunday School lessons suitable for adults, young people and children must be written. The reforms were put into practice immediately. A superintendent was elected, José Fernandes Braga; twenty-six teachers were chosen, five of whom were to serve in the daughter church in Niteroi; and the outlines of the first series of lessons were prepared. And so, on 16 July 1871, there began what was to be the most popular and most frequented gathering of the week in the churches as a whole in Brazil – the Sunday School. On that first day in the Fluminense Church some 200 were enrolled. It was a tremendous step forward. The people already had the Bible and were reading it, but what they lacked in systematic study of the Bible the Sunday School supplied, geared to each age-group. When that humble group of believers met in their reorganized Sunday School they little thought that they were establishing something that would be vital to the growth of the church in Brazil.

Mrs Kalley was anxious to organize a women's society but, as she herself wrote, 'For a long time I hesitated to do so, since the church people assured me that to do this would be against the culture of the country, seeing that no woman was allowed to go out in the street alone: she must be chaperoned by a male member of her family.' 'Now', Mrs Kalley added, 'we have three German women in the church who refuse to submit to such restrictions. I resolved to found the society first having ascertained that eleven women favoured the idea. At the second meeting we had a total of fourteen, and I believe that more will unite with us in the near future.' Once again the Kalleys made a contribution of inestimable value to the Brazilian church. The Ladies' Meeting, the *Sociedade de Senhoras*, is an essential element in every local church: it is often called, and in most cases rightly so, the 'right arm of the church'.

Constant activity

In the heat and bustle of Rio, and with the heavy work-load, Dr Kalley's health continued to give his wife and friends cause for anxiety. Towards the end of July they left Rio for a short break. They travelled on the newly inaugurated railway to Palmeiras, a beautiful location situated high in the mountain range, Serra do Mar, far above the steaming heat of the city. Even there the doctor allowed himself no respite from his evangelistic zeal. He records that he spoke 'to a group of coloured people and nine of them came to the hotel that night to hear more of the gospel'. Next day he conversed with the station-master and at night the man, accompanied by seven others, came to learn what the Bible taught about salvation. Seventeen coloured people also attended.'

The Fluminense Church settled down to a revised weekly routine: Sunday – Sunday School and worship services; Monday – Music Class and the learning of new hymns; Tuesday – Ladies' Meeting; Wednesday – mid-week service; Friday – special training classes for Sunday School teachers. In addition there were evangelistic meetings in different suburbs and in Niteroi. It was a time of constant, incessant activity.

When at home in Rio the doctor received a constant stream of visitors, church members and others seeking his help and advice. Then, too, there was the flow of correspondence, and he had no secretary! A lengthy correspondence ensued as the result of Mr Holden's expressing his doubts as to 'imputed righteousness', doubts which the doctor sought to dispel.

From Portugal came reports sent by colporteurs and other workers, tales of persecution and hardships, all in an effort to give the Bible to the people. One of them, who had been converted in Brazil, wrote, 'We see here in Portugal the good fruit produced by the sowing of the seed in Brazil.' Another wrote from the jail in Santa Marota: 'Here I am: the jailer took away my books, three letters I had in my pocket and all my money. My situation is desperate – without money, far from friends, and alone in this dungeon. The chief of police and the magistrates have threatened me, saying that I ought to be burnt alive in the market-place for all to see. I have already been in other jails in Traz dos Montes, but in spite of it all I managed to sell four thousand copies of Scripture. I fear, however, that many were gathered up and burnt. I do not know when I will get out again . . . I must confess that my faith has faltered . . . so much persecution in this, the worst part of the kingdom. Signed, Manoel Francisco da Silva.'

Still another, Patrocínio by name, wrote that he had been in Ponte de Sôr, after being released from custody in Figueira do Vinho. He still had with him two boxes of Scriptures and was selling them in the market at Cabaças e Thomar. Later, this same colporteur reported: 'In this congregation [Olhão in the Algarve] some thirty people were in a meeting when the priests incited fanatics to rip the doors off their hinges and beat up any they found in the congregation. These poor creatures were then left to starve. No one would sell them anything. Some, in order to survive, returned to the Catholic Church, to mass and confession, but even so they were badly ill-treated, even in the church building itself.' These reports show how far-ranging were these Portuguese colporteurs in their outreach. They persisted doggedly on their way through town and village, in spite of persecution and imprisonment.

Letters arrived too from Madeira and Illinois informing the doctor of the progress of the gospel and the difficulties encountered. Each letter received a faithful hand-written reply.

In yet another sphere Dr and Mrs Kalley were active, and that was among the English-speaking community, both British and American. In their spacious, hospitable home, they entertained high-ranking officials and others from both countries. These social contacts were opportunities for witness, quiet and effective, yet without embarrassment to the guests. Then, too, the doctor took services for British expatriates in private homes when invited to do so. Even the Anglican chaplain was greatly helped and encouraged by him, and as a result stated in a letter that 'he would endeavour to speak to the congregation with greater clarity of our ruin in Adam, and our redemption in Christ'.

One of the second-generation believers in the Fluminense Church, Dr Henrique de Souza Jardim, testified: 'My father always said that Dr Kalley won the hearts of all who approached him. He spoke gently and humbly, yet firmly when he spoke a word of exhortation to someone or replied to a question put to him. And, even if the one to whom he spoke answered him back harshly or rudely, the doctor did not alter his tone of voice, but continued to speak in a friendly way. The result was that some of his interlocutors were enlightened, and having before them such a living example of Christlikeness, they themselves became firm in the faith and trustworthy leaders in the church. The Portuguese, especially when returning to Portugal, either on a visit or to reside, had the firm conviction that they must preach the gospel to their fellow-countrymen.'

Mrs Kalley adds her testimony: 'During our journeyings what perhaps struck me most in my beloved husband was his remarkable power of dealing with souls in every possible circumstance. I often timed him, and in three minutes from the moment some inquisitive passenger accosted him with the most ordinary questions, he would frequently be engaged in close Christian talk, and though his companion often looked surprised or puzzled, I do not remember a single instance when this was resented. It was the same through his long life. I often felt that his special gift lay in his power of close personal dealings. Often he was a silent member of mere general society, but one-to-one never seemed to be conscious of difficulty in speaking with the utmost directness for his Lord.'

A change of pastor

In a letter to Dr Kalley late in December 1871, Mr Holden informed him that he would not be returning to continue his ministry in the Fluminense Church. He gave three valid reasons for his decision. Firstly, he could not, in all conscience, accept that a pastor should receive remuneration for his services. Secondly, doctrinal differences existed between him and the doctor. Thirdly, he wrote, 'I could not return to Rio in the faith that I was being lead thither by God. I have decided tonight to resign my pastorate and the service of the Bible Society.' When Dr Kalley informed the church of Mr Holden's decision there was universal consternation. Church members could not believe that the decision was final. 'When the letter from Mr Holden was read out in the church, expressions of grief dissolved into floods of tears.' The news saddened the brethren extremely since Mr Holden was greatly esteemed for his zeal, his dedication to the service of the church, his untiring devotion and his innate friendliness and courtesy.

The church resolved to send a manifesto to Mr Holden, expressing their deep regret at his decision, which they sincerely hoped would still be open to reconsideration, and to thank him for his extremely fruitful ministry among them. Shortly afterwards Mr Holden wrote to Dr Kalley from Guernsey informing him that he had been in contact with Mr Darby and Mr Kelly, and was convinced that the doctrines and practices of the Plymouth Brethren were in full accord with Scripture and that he now belonged to the Assembly. He added a note to the effect that Dr Kalley had been mistaken in his assessment of J.N. Darby: 'From from being a "pope", he is a humble, courteous servant of God.'

To encourage the church, though, preparations for João dos Santos' pastoral studies in Spurgeon's College were nearing completion. He was taking special classes in English and winding up his business affairs in Rio as a partner in a shoe shop. Finance was a serious problem. Dr Kalley wrote to Spurgeon: 'Sixteen years have passed since I began my work in Brazil, and the church has grown slowly. At present there are a hundred and fifty members and all exceedingly poor. I myself pay all the expenses for the upkeep of the church: water, light, etc. As to João Manoel Gonçalves dos Santos ... I will pay his return fare to England, as also the greater part of his upkeep and studies.' Santos finally sailed on 8 August 1872. He was then thirty years old and after study would serve the Fluminense Church for thirty-nine years and, as agent of the Bible Society, all the churches in Brazil.

Discussions on baptism

The question of infant baptism continued to agitate the church meetings. For a long time Dona Christina Fernandes Braga, wife of José Luiz Fernandes Braga, had expressed the desire to become a member of the Fluminense Church, but had been barred from doing so because the church ruled that she must submit to believers' baptism, administered by sprinkling. Dona Christina was of German extraction and had been in Mrs Kalley's Sunday School class in Petropolis as a young girl. She had been baptized in infancy by the Lutheran pastor there. She owed her conversion to the Kalleys but had persistently refused rebaptism on the grounds that her christening was authentic baptism. Finally, she did yield to pressure and accepted rebaptism and was then admitted to the Lord's Table also.

A further case arose which, for a lengthy period, defied solution. A daughter of Gama, Maria Julia, had been baptized in infancy by Dr Kalley, according to the rites of the Presbyterian Church of which the doctor was at that time still a member. The discussion at successive church meetings was heated. A compromise was finally reached, probably in deference to the doctor in his dilemma. The church decided that it should be left to the conscience of the candidate in this particular case, whether she would seek believer's baptism or not, 'it being understood that the church did not approve by this act of tolerance the baptism of infants'. She was, therefore, received into membership. This precedent did, however, become a principle : infant baptism practised by other Protestant churches was acceptable, but not that of the Roman church.

Schools and medical work

On several occasions the question of starting a church school was raised. It was not easy to open a school in the city as imperial permission had to be obtained for the school to have the liberty to choose its own teachers. It was decided, however, to apply for permission to found an independent school, especially for the children of believers. The school would function in the premises at the back of the church, and tuition would be free of charge; voluntary contributions would finance the venture. The school began to function on 17 June 1872, but it was not a success owing to financial problems and the difficulty of finding dedicated teachers.

Early in 1873 yet again a severe epidemic of yellow fever swept through the city. The doctor wrote an article in the press in an endeavour to teach people preventive measures and, as might be expected, seeking to comfort the bereaved. The church also appointed sick visitors – those who would visit sufferers in their own homes. Pamphlets on the scourge were also printed and widely distributed. The crisis passed. The church, however, continued to run a clinic for the poor, of whom there were many in the vicinity.

22.
Church – planting in Recife

Brazil has always fascinated the explorer. Its vastness, variety, wealth and, above all, its mystery, have enticed and challenged adventurers to discover its secrets down through the centuries. During the eighteenth century Brazilian explorers known as *Bandeirantes*, based on São Paulo, made sorties into the distant fastnesses of the hinterland in search of slaves, gold, precious stones and, especially, the fabled Mountain of Emeralds. It was they who explored and eventually sparsely populated vast areas of the interior. In the nineteenth century naturalists, mainly British and most of them emissaries of Kew Gardens, pushed their way through the rain forests of the Amazon, and on through the bushlands of the Central Plateau, discovering and cataloguing the infinite riches of Brazilian flora and fauna.

British and Brazilian friends of the Kalleys must have insisted with them that they visit the most civilized areas of the country's interior, in order to discover for themselves the Brazil that 'lies beyond the mountains'. By the second half of the century British agricultural and mining interests had spread westwards, deep into the hinterland, forming small enclaves of the British way of life, even in such an exotic environment. Miss North, in her travels through Brazil, was the welcome guest in such areas, as, for example, at a gold mine run by the British in the very heart of Brazil. The Kalleys would have been welcome guests too, but such invitations they courteously but firmly refused. They were single-minded: they had a mission to fulfil and little time in which to do it. There was an immediacy and urgency about their God-given task that demanded all their time, energies and means too. Nothing would divert them.

A wealthy English industrialist offered them tempting concessions if they would move their sphere of labours to the Amazon and devote themselves to the betterment of the Indians. They refused and continued to confine their activities to the immediate neighbourhood of the Bay of Guanabara – Rio de Janeiro and Niteroi.

A notable exception

The doctor was not an itinerant missionary like his American Presbyterian colleagues became. He believed that the actual work of evangelism could be done most effectively by nationals, such as Gama, Jardim, Vianna, men of simple faith who knew how to reach the hearts of the people. He made one notable exception, however, and that was to accept an invitation to visit Recife, the capital city of Pernambuco in north-east Brazil. Persecution there was threatening to close down the work altogether.

The first colporteur to visit Recife was a deacon of the Fluminense Church, Manoel José da Silva Vianna, in 1868. Vianna was a Portuguese of humble origin who learned to read at the age of forty. He first became interested in the Scriptures through a member of the church but it took the tragic death of a daughter in Portugal to 'shock' him into faith. He was baptized in 1866 and two years later felt the call of God to dedicate his life to colportage. At Dr Kalley's request he undertook to go to Recife.

Vianna was a man of a very different calibre to Thomas Goulart, the colporteur who took the city of Salvador, Bahia, by storm. He slipped quietly and unostentatiously into Recife. One who knew him well described him as middle-aged, bald, bearded, very friendly and very tolerant, but with a strength of will-power that could be goaded into obstinacy. Nothing could divert him from the way he was set to go. 'With a bag in his left hand and a couple of books in his right, he can-vassed the city – always smiling, always offering his books and, when occasion arose, willing to give an explanation of the contents of the gospel he offered.' What the Dutch had failed to do by sheer weight of military might and political power, to 'give the Bible to the people', Vianna did by the

God-honoured method of colportage. Interestingly enough, Vianna arrived in Recife exactly 200 years after the Dutch had surrendered the city to the victorious Brazilians!

A celebrated historian, Dr Vincente Ferrer de Barros Araujo, a native of Recife, and a staunch defender of the 'Calvinists', as the Protestants were sometimes called, declared that a bust of Vianna ought to stand in a prominent place in the city as a worthy tribute to the man who first introduced the gospel to Pernambuco and the north-east.

The town of Recife

Recife, so called after the reef which runs parallel to the coast at that point, was a city of some 50,000 inhabitants in the middle of the nineteenth century. The port, built opposite a break in the reef, an excellent if narrow entrance to a commodious and safe harbour, was one of the busiest in Brazil. Alas, the city itself had degenerated into an urban slum; little of its former glory remained. The streets were unpaved, with open sewers running down the centre. Some streets, near the centre, did have two-storied houses with Portuguese tiled façades and balconies on the first floor, but for the most part they were lined with one-storey buildings of a nondescript nature. There were, of course, the usual number of churches, mostly baroque in style, characteristic of the bigger towns in Brazil, but other imposing public buildings were non-existent.

Charles Waterton, an English naturalist who visited Recife in 1816, extolled the beauty of the surroundings: 'The two rivers meandering their way through the city, and the inlets from the sea, making the city a veritable Venice, so numerous were the bridges', but further notes, 'When you see the port of Pernambuco full of ships from all nations, when you know that the rich commodities of Africa, Asia and Europe, are brought to it, when you see the immense quantities of dye-wood, cotton, fresh fruits and other goods pouring into the town, you are apt to wonder at the little attention these people pay to common comforts which one always expects to find in an opulent city. As you walk the streets the appearance of the houses is not so much in their favour. Some are very high and some are very low: some newly whitewashed and others stained and mouldy, as though they had no owners. The impurities from the houses, and the accumulation of litter from the beasts of burden, are unpleasant sights for the passing stranger.' Waterton did, however, confess that after living there for several weeks the unpleasant sights and smells were no longer noticed!

An interesting sidelight is thrown on the traffic in slaves in Brazil. Waterton wanted to travel north from Recife to São Luiz de Maranhão, but found it almost impossible to get a suitable passage. So many of the boats travelling from port to port were slave ships. He described the decks as being crowded with human cargo: slaves to be offered to the highest bidder at any port of call. In Recife, as in Rio, the Kalleys would have encountered an abnormal number of slaves going about their menial tasks in circumstances of the utmost degradation. Mules and slaves, on an equal footing, were employed in intensive labour on the sugar plantations within the environs of the city.

The people of Recife

And what of the people in general? Known as *nortistas* – 'northeasterners' – they lived not only in Recife itself but were scattered throughout the hinterland, the *sertão*, in a vast area covering various states – Alagoas, Pernambuco, Paraíba, Rio Grande do Norte and Ceará. Dr Gilberto Freire, one of the leading intellectuals of Brazil, himself a *nortista*, declared that Brazil does not form part of Latin America. He based his claim on the fact that the Brazilian, in contrast to the inhabitants of other South American republics, is the product of the intermingling of three distinct races: the Indian of the rain forests – the original inhabitants; the Portuguese – the *conquistadores*; and the African slave – imported labour. In the rest of South America such a thorough admixture of races did not occur; they are essentially of Latin origin with, in the western republics, a tinge of Inca blood. Freire added that the *nortistas* retain their racial origins almost intact; the 'bleaching process' of the nineteenth century passed them by, since the European immigrants – Swiss, German, Italian –

established themselves in the fertile and prosperous south. The *nortistas* are of a fiercely independent spirit, as shown in their ousting of the Dutch invaders in the seventeenth century. To quote Freire, 'The victory awakened in them the spirit of nationalism and "motivism" so characteristic of the Pernambucanos.' In the years that followed, that same turbulent, independent spirit was the cause of many a revolt and political upheaval. For example, a year before Brazil's Declaration of Independence in 1822, the *Pernambucanos* had already concluded a treaty with the Portuguese authorities for them to abdicate all their rights and withdraw their armed forces! It constituted a virtual declaration of independence – Pernambuco was no longer part of a Portuguese colony – and the more radical elements endeavoured to force the issue and declare Pernambuco independent of Brazil too!

Another factor has contributed to the independence and toughness of the *nortista* – the harshness of the climate and environment. The whole of the *sertão* was always plagued by a cycle of droughts, occurring more or less once every decade. For two, three, or even four years no rains fell, crops failed and no harvests were reaped. It meant for them starvation and the survival of the fittest. After two seasons without rain and with all hope of a crop gone, the *sertanejos* would begin their long trek, hundreds of miles to the towns in the coastal region. *En route* children died, and pitiful remnants of once large families, emaciated to skin and bone, dragged themselves along the trails.

The gospel comes to Recife

To these *nortistas* Vianna took the gospel. During his first short visit in 1868, followed by a more prolonged stay in 1871, Vianna found the prospects for the gospel to be good. He encountered, as he fully expected, a forbidding wall of ignorance and superstition, deeply rooted traditionalism and fanatical observance of religious festivals, but he shrewdly observed cracks in the barriers of opposition. Not everyone rejected his offer of the Scriptures, nor refused to hear his reasoned explanations. Some listened intently to what he had to say, and bought copies of the Scriptures and read them for themselves. A few professed conversion and began to meet regularly for Bible study. Seeing these signs of blessing, Vianna hurried back to Rio and obtained from Dr Kalley leave to move to Recife with his wife and family.

They rented a house in the poorer quarters of the city, near the docks. Vianna wrote to Dr Kalley enthusiastically: 'We received a tremendous welcome from the brethren here. On Sunday, 1st December, we held a meeting in a house – my own house not being ready yet to serve as a meeting-place. I bought benches, lamps, and yesterday we had our first meeting in our home. Nineteen were present in the morning and twenty-seven at night. Seventeen were enrolled in the Sunday School.' Family worship, held daily, attracted the attention of the neighbours. The hymn tunes were so bright and the words so easy to understand that by hymn-singing alone the gospel was being preached. Gradually the congregation increased in size.

Harassment

Colportage was not easy; it demanded stamina. Vianna went from house to house, street to street, to the market-place, in fact to any place where people were to be found. As time went on he extended his colportage work to places up-country. There, in the provinces just as in the city, he suffered. He was constantly harassed. The mobs hurled insults at him, grabbed his bag and scattered his books on the ground, and then rendered them unreadable by trampling on them and rubbing them in the dust. At the instigation of the local priest the police confiscated any books he still had, undertook to turn a blind eye to the violence of the mob and even to incarcerate the intrepid colporteur. People were forbidden, on pain of excommunication, to read the Bible or even possess one. The word '*P-r-o-t-e-s-t-a-n-t-e*' was used to good effect. If pronounced slowly and deliberately it lends itself to an unparalleled expression of hatred.

The persecution followed the usual pattern which Dr Kalley himself had experienced in Madeira. When it became obvious that threats of excommunication did not deter everybody from reading the Bible, the clergy sought to prove that the Bible was false. To them, the only legitimate Bible was the Roman Catholic version, translated from the Latin, and with the imprimatur of the ecclesiastical authorities. They declared that there was no need for the laity to read the Bible at all, since the sole authenticated interpreter of Scripture was the Holy Mother Church and that church could be trusted to transmit any Bible knowledge the ordinary man might need. If any further information was desired then the priest could be asked. In any case, they reasoned, the Bible was read every day in mass, therefore by attending mass the people would hear the gospel. No mention was made of the fact that the mass was in Latin!

The Bible under attack

What had happened in Salvador, though, was repeated in Recife. Men who were well-read and liberal in their outlook sprang to the defence of Vianna. They sought to prove two things: that there was only one true Bible, whether Protestant or Catholic, in which case the Catholic Church was not the sole interpreter of biblical truth; that the common man had the right to read the Bible for himself and to 'read, learn and inwardly digest' gospel truth. Articles in defence of Vianna appeared in the press, and pamphlets on the veracity of the 'Vianna Bible' were widely distributed. The groundwork for such a spirited defence was prepared already because Kidder in his travels through Brazil, some thirty years earlier, had paid a brief visit to Recife and while there distributed copies of the Scriptures. The clergy had immediately inveighed against these 'falsified Bibles', declaring them to be not only false but also truncated. The priests had aroused the ire of one of the most renowned protagonists of religious tolerance, General José Ignácio Ribeiro de Abreu e Lima Filho (1796-1864). The general was a *Pernambucano* and a typical *nortista,* an independent. Besides being a distinguished military man he was a professor of repute and an ardent reformer. His liberal views, boldly expressed, had already proved unacceptable to the Brazilian authorities, and he had suffered imprisonment and exile.

While in exile the general had played an active part in the

wars of independence both in Venezuela and Columbia. He
was later reinstated and returned home to Recife. None was
better suited either by temperament or by learning to defend
Kidder's Bible. He wrote a well-researched defence of the
Bible, citing Greek and Hebrew where necessary, as also the
church fathers. He used the pseudonym *O Cristão Velho* – the
'aged Christian' – and his reasoning was irrefutable. Since he
was such a public figure, made famous by his exploits in the
armed forces, in literature and in politics – and, incredible
though it may seem, an ardent Roman Catholic – his word
carried weight. The church never forgave him and when he
died the Bishop of Olinda refused permission to bury him in
consecrated ground. The British opened the gates of their
Anglican Church graveyard and he was buried there with all
the honours those Protestant foreigners could pay him.
The incident aroused the anger of the emperor and he
publicly rebuked the bishop. The same bishop was afterwards sentenced to four years' imprisonment for further
misdemeanours!

When, therefore, Vianna's Bible was attacked the memory
of Abreu e Lima was still vivid in the minds of the more
enlightened of the local population.

Presbyterian missionaries in Recife

By 1873 Vianna had a sizeable congregation gathering for
worship each Sunday. The first Presbyterian missionary to
Recife, the Rev. John Rockwell Smith, an American, had
recently arrived. He is revered by the Presbyterian Church in
Brazil as the pioneer missionary of the north and north-
eastern territories and as head of the seminary in which the
first generation of national ministers received their training.
His goatee beard gained for his followers the onerous title of
bode – goat! He described a service conducted by Vianna
which he attended shortly after his arrival: 'The first Sunday
morning meeting I attended went as follows: hymn, prayer,
reading of the first three chapters of Peter's first epistle,
accompanied by a running commentary, hymn and prayer.
The whole service occupied about two hours. The small congregation, with Bibles open, was very keen, most attentive

and appeared to be very devout. Perhaps they may well serve as a challenge to many congregations at home. At the close of the meeting all came to shake me by the hand, one old fellow taking my hand in both of his. Vianna is very pleased at my having come, and when I told him that I was expecting Mr and Mrs Boyle to arrive he assured me that there was plenty of room in town for three churches... These are the first-fruits in the zone.'

Services suspended

Dr Kalley had accepted Vianna's appeal to visit Recife but persecution threatened to close the church before he arrived. A police inspector brutally forced his way into a service and ordered all such meetings to cease. In vain Vianna appealed to the chief of police: the man refused to intervene. Vianna carried his case to the state governor, and when he refused to guarantee the constitutional right of freedom of worship Vianna threatened to appeal to the imperial authorities in Rio de Janeiro. It was no longer possible to hold services: the police had sealed the doors of the meeting room. Mr Rockwell Smith had, by this time, learned Portuguese and was ready to begin preaching. He personally interviewed the governor and was assured of four things: the constitution warranted his absolute freedom to propagate his religious ideas; he could hold services in buildings which did not resemble a church; he could reach out into the state schools if invited to do so; he could hold family worship in his own home. While with the governor Mr Rockwell Smith took the opportunity to plead Vianna's cause, and so a few weeks before Dr Kalley arrived the interdict was lifted. The congregation was then able to resume its normal life and witness.

The whole incident aroused public interest. The press made banner headlines of the arbitrary action of the police, and the Jesuit news-sheet vituperated Vianna and all his works. Since, among other things, Vianna was accused of maligning the Virgin someone in Rio outlined a doctrinal statement of Protestant beliefs which a daily paper in Recife gladly published. The Masons and the bishop were drawn in and became embroiled in heated discussion. Such publicity was good for the gospel and prepared the way for Dr Kalley's visit.

The doctor's visit

There was only one way to travel from Rio to Recife, and that was by boat as no through-road existed. Paddle steamers plied between Brazilian ports, greatly facilitating both commerce and travel. On 20 September 1873, the Kalleys embarked in Rio and eight days later arrived in Recife. Accommodation was not easy to find, since there were no hotels in the city and any type of guest house was disreputable. Hearing of the difficulty, the American missionaries immediately offered them hospitality.

The small congregation in Recife was now meeting in the workshop of a basket-weaver, Alexandre Soares. Mrs Kalley was distressed at the way hymns were sung – slowly, out of tune, with wrong notes, and yet with great gusto! She set about remedying the situation – not an easy task! Dr Kalley's first care was to minister to the believers, some thirty in number. He preached and taught as and when opportunity offered. With Vianna and his wife the Kalleys compiled a list of candidates for baptism – the first church meeting held in Recife. During the next few days they interviewed them one by one, and eventually reached the conclusion that only twelve were ready for baptism. A minute, recording the decision and the twelve names, was registered. Dr Kalley made a few formal visits; to the municipal authorities to consult the register of marriages of non-Catholics; to the British consul, Captain Doyle; to a Miss Davies, who kept an English guest house. With a single eye to his main task, that of making Christ known in Recife, he cast his net wide. He asked Miss Davies's permission to use her house as a venue for a lecture to British and Americans on the Holy Land. Some forty people heard the doctor's talk on Palestine and, incidentally, a few gospel truths also. The doctor then sought means to repeat the lecture in Portuguese for the general public. The difficulty was to find a hall sufficiently large. Eventually he arranged to give his talk in a theatre and since the lecture had been widely publicized, the building was packed.

One of the leading figures in literature and politics, Dr Vincente Ferrer de Barros Wanderley Araujo, was present in the audience and was greatly impressed by what he heard, as also by the speaker himself. Years later he wrote a learned and reasoned defence of the believers in Pernambuco at a time of severe persecution. At the other end of the social scale, a young Portuguese, Manoel de Souza Andrade, recently arrived from the Azores and employed as a theatre attendant, heard the gospel that night and shortly afterwards was converted. He was destined to become a leading elder in the church. An interesting side-light to his conversion is that when he went home with a Bible and announced to his mother, a widow, that he was now a believer, the stout old lady, a devout Catholic, was so incensed that she seized a broom and beat her son until she broke the handle over his back! He quietly submitted to the beating but after it was all over and his mother had recovered her breath, he announced: 'Mother, you can beat me, but one thing you cannot do and that is beat the gospel out of me!'

The church is set up

Of the twelve candidates accepted for baptism three couples were living together without being married. Before baptism they needed to legalize their situation, so, exercising the right which Brazilian law gave him, Dr Kalley, as pastor, conducted the wedding ceremony and had the documents duly registered with the authorities. On 19 October 1873, Dr Kalley organized the congregation into a church, the *Igreja Evangélica Pernambucana,* the first indigenous evangelical church in the north-east of Brazil, and the second in the country. That day the twelve were baptized. Immediately after baptism and the formal organization of the new church, the Lord's Supper was celebrated, and the converts initiated into the true 'communion of saints'.

With all this publicity and activity it was evident that larger premises for the church were urgently needed. A much bigger house was rented and furnished with the essentials for holding services. At the mid-week meeting Dr Kalley conducted yet another marriage ceremony: two of those recently baptized were married. He later described what happened: 'The room was filled with people who attended quietly and reverently, in contrast to the uproar in the street outside. The police were summoned and they pushed their way into the room. Ignorant of the decree of 17 October 1863, which permitted the marriage of non-Catholics by a competent person – a pastor – they declared that nobody had the right to conduct such marriage ceremonies. The authorities made no move to disperse the crowd and when I went out, accompanied by my wife, we were followed by a mob of between 500 and 600 people making cat-calls, shouting obscenities, showering us with dust, and throwing stones, finally making us seek refuge, kindly offered and made available to us in a house in the Rua dos Caldeiros. The street was filled with the uproar of the mob until well after midnight.' The following night there were further demonstrations and windows in the meeting hall were smashed.

Dr Kalley interviewed the chief of police. The following Sunday, the chief of police, with a strong contingent of police officers, attended the morning service and 'not even a dog barked'! Later in the week when the police were not present there was further trouble, and windows were smashed. The outcome was that the police promised to maintain law and order in future. Further meetings were held under the watchful eye of the authorities and persecution ceased. Throughout that month of trying experiences the Kalleys received the gracious help of the Boyles, who would have done more had they been fluent in Portuguese. On 10 November the Kalleys embarked on an English boat, the *Magellan* for Rio and home.

They left Recife with a sense of 'mission accomplished'. The Pernambucano Church had been duly organized and the believers heartened and encouraged; persecution had been endured and demonstrated to be futile – the church was strengthened by it; the authorities, the chief of police and the state govenor had been interviewed and had guaranteed that freedom of worship would be maintained; cordial relationships had been established with the American Presbyterians. The gospel cause had taken root in the north-east and nothing could impede its growth.

23.
Last days in Brazil

Back home in Rio the Kalleys picked up the threads of routine life and work. An eventful year, 1873, was drawing to a close.

From the doctor's pen there still flowed a constant stream of articles for the press, pamphlets and, above all, letters. News from Illinois was disturbing. The Madeiran churches there were deeply divided: schismatic influences had wrought havoc in the fellowship of believers. Dr Kalley was deeply grieved that such things should be taking place and wrote pastoral letters in an effort to heal the divisions. He was reliving Paul's experiences with the Corinthian church. By contrast, there was good news from Madeira. The remnants left after the persecutions of the 1840s had formed themselves into a church and were bearing an effective witness. The brethren in Pernambuco, though, were experiencing difficulties. The Bible Society, which was partly responsible for financing Vianna, demanded that he give more time to colportage and less to the church, threatening him with relocation. The good offices of the doctor were sought to work out a compromise, and as a result Vianna stayed on in Recife. In the Rio church two of the leading members proved to be trouble-makers, and although they left the church and joined the Presbyterians, they still continued to create problems. Mr Holden had spent a few months in the city after his defection to the Plymouth Brethren, and such was his influence among members of the Fluminense Church that some left to join the assembly he founded in the city. In justice to Mr Holden it must be said that this was not deliberate proselytizing on his part, but the result of the esteem in which he had been held by certain members of the Fluminense Church. In the process of time, however, most of those who had left became disillusioned and returned to the Fluminense Church. The care of all the churches weighed heavily on the doctor's shoulders.

Through it all Mrs Kalley continued to be a help-meet for him. For some years she had made herself responsible to oversee the work of the colporteurs: she received their reports, supervised their finances, attended to their stocks of books and gave them every encouragement in their difficult task. For them persecution, beatings and even imprisonment were a way of life. She also helped lay preachers to prepare their sermons, making sure that they really expounded the text. On occasions she supplied her husband with suggested outlines for his sermons. Her early training in dealing with men in her Bible class in Torquay stood her in good stead in the highly chauvinistic social climate of Brazil. In a very practical way she sought to lessen her husband's work-load.

Teresopolis

Towards the end of the year, 1874, the pressures of work, combined with the oppressive heat of the city, obliged the Kalleys to take another break. They went to Teresopolis in the Organ Mountains to the west of Petropolis, where a wealthy and gregarious Englishman, Mr Lowe, had built 'holiday chalets' on his vast estate. The journey up there was even more demanding than that to Petropolis, since there was no railway across the marshes. That part of the journey, from the head of the bay to the foot of the mountains, was done in a mule-drawn vehicle. The remainder, a trail winding its way up the steep mountain slope and round the foot of the gigantic granite peak known as 'the Finger of God', was accomplished on horseback. The views from the higher reaches of the trail, overlooking the bay, were breath-taking, said to be unsurpassed anywhere else in the world. Such scenes would rejoice Mrs Kalley's artistic nature and compensate for the exhaustion of the climb. The trail was in the process of being widened and so the doctor passed the time of day with the gang of men working there. A few days later he returned to their encampment to distribute gospel literature and chat to them about the claims of Christ. The impact must have been very great, that a doctor, one of the upper class, should take the trouble of riding down the mountain to chat with them! That was typical of the man: he could 'gossip the gospel' with men at all levels, from the emperor to the road-mender.

In spite of the fact that Teresopolis was on a main 'highway' to the hinterland, with a constant stream of mule-trains passing through, it was situated in untamed territory. The rain forests surrounding the clearings were no longer peopled with Indians – they had been driven further inland – but the superabundant flora and fauna of Brazil were evident on every hand. In such novel surroundings and invigorating climate the doctor and his wife rested and recuperated. They were, of course, in constant touch with the church in the city below, couriers carrying letters to and fro.

Crisis in Brazil

After several weeks they returned home. The year 1875 was proving to be a difficult one for Brazil. Brazilian history is studded with times of crisis and 1875 was one of them. The country was still reeling from the long-drawn-out war with Paraguay (1864-70), a struggle which had cost the country thousands of lives and had brought it to the brink of bankruptcy. Various pressure groups were making their influence increasingly felt. In politics the 'republican party' was becoming more vocal, and the emperor, characteristically, was lenient towards those who opposed him. When he appointed a new minister, on one occasion, someone remonstrated with him: 'But he is a Republican!' True to his nature the emperor replied: 'He is the best man for the job, whatever his politics.'

The anti-slave movement was sensing victory and increasing its pressure, but the most significant feature of the crisis was the growing rift between church and state. The state had always sought to curb the power of the church, not provoking an all-out confrontation, but by implementing measures which ensured that the church would not take complete control of the country. The emperor and his more enlightened ministers detested the political intrigues of the Roman Catholic Church and exposed them. The Catholic Church was even more incensed against the state for its leniency towards 'Protestant intruders'. They looked askance at the friendship between the Kalleys and the royal household and Court. The Bishop of Olinda was imprisoned for four years, Jesuits were expelled, and repressive measures introduced to restrain recalcitrant clergy. Pundits avowed that the separation between church and state could not be delayed for long. This tolerance at official levels, however, did not eliminate harassment and persecution of believers at local levels. The Rev. Blackford, in the interior of the state of São Paulo, experienced opposition similar to that experienced by Dr Kalley in Rio de Janeiro, Niteroi and Recife. But the newly-founded church, although a small minority, was alive and growing.

Hospitality

The Kalleys had no children of their own, but about this time they adopted a Brazilian boy, João Gomes da Rocha and, later, a girl, Silvania Azara, or Sia, as she was called in the familiarity of the home. There was a constant stream of guests into that hospitable home: at the midday meal, colporteurs or ordinary folk from the church; at dinner, diplomats from British, American or other embassies, visitors from abroad, Brazilian friends. Mrs Kalley was a gracious hostess, notably when she presided at afternoon tea parties for her friends.

Brazilian pastors trained

The programme for the training of the Brazilian ministry was now taking shape. João Manoel Gonçalves dos Santos was about to finish his course at Spurgeon's Pastors' College, and two young men from the Recife area also felt the call of God to the ministry, Aderito Gomes da Silva and Leônides Franciso da Silva. Dr Kalley wrote to his friend, Dr Grattan Guinness, who had recently founded the East End Training Institute, asking for his help. This was readily granted and the two candidates sailed for London. Aderito Gomes did not return to Brazil, but stayed on in Britain; it was Leônides who was to become one of the leading pastors in the Kalley churches.

At the end of the college term João Gonçalves dos Santos began his journey back to Brazil. Dr Kalley suggested that he stop off at Recife in order to minister to the church there. This he did, staying for a whole month. He finally reached Rio at the end of September and was given a very warm welcome by the church. Shortly afterwards he was elected co-pastor, and duly registered to perform marriage ceremonies. He soon proved himself to be an effective, caring pastor.

With the arrival of the new pastor the Kalleys decided that the time had come for them to retire and return to Britain. The church was thriving with 120 communicants; a Brazilian pastor was installed; here was a mature and disciplined body of laymen; an on-going evangelistic outreach was being made into the suburbs of Rio and over the bay in Niteroi and, through colportage, into the vast hinterland. The future of the church was assured. The hot season was approaching and so the doctor and his wife journeyed up to Petropolis for a prolonged stay. From there they wrote to the church intimating their intention to retire to Scotland. While in Petropolis they took the opportunity of calling on the emperor and took leave of him and his wife. Preparations for leaving were well under way.

The Twenty-Eight Articles

During the relatively short period of twenty-one years that he had lived and laboured in Brazil the doctor had laid the foundations for a continuing work of the gospel. He had given the Bible to the people, trained converts to witness to the gospel, not only by preaching but also by their lives, prepared a group of stalwart lay-preachers, begun the preparation of a national ministry, given the church in Brazil a hymnbook and had instigated a definite interpretation of the Brazilian Constitution as touching religious freedom. There was, however, one thing that yet remained to be done: that was to give the church a doctrinal statement of faith. For some time Dr Kalley had been preparing a statement of faith to be incorporated into the constitution of the churches in Rio and Recife. He submitted a draft copy to the church meetings and, with only slight amendments, it was approved in July 1876. It is known as *Os Vinte-Oito Artigos da Breve Exposição – The Twenty-Eight Articles of the Shorter Catechism*. In reality the document was more than the setting forth, in an ordered manner, of the cardinal doctrines of faith – the triune God, man, salvation in Christ, the church, the consummation of all things – it was Dr Kalley's seal to all he had accomplished. Just as the affixing of a seal authenticated a document, so the *Twenty-Eight Articles* were the doctor's seal and signature to his work as being Bible-based, Christ-centred and God-glorifying. This authentic seal would be passed on to succeeding generations of Kalley churches.

In June Mrs Kalley conducted the last meeting of the Ladies' Society before leaving and, on 2 July, Dr Kalley conducted the final communion service. Eight days later they embarked for home amid emotional scenes so characteristic of leave-taking in Brazil. Under divine compulsion they had gone to Brazil, the land of the Christless cross; they now left it with the true cross firmly embedded in its soil.

Part III
Mission Accomplished

24.
'Green pastures'

After their arrival back in Scotland, Dr and Mrs Kalley fixed their residence in Edinburgh. They bought a site in the Merchiston district and built their own house in Tipperlyne Road. In memory of the green countryside around Petropolis they called it 'Campo Verde' – 'Green Pastures'. It would also recall Psalm 23 in the Portuguese version. Both the doctor and his wife, with their rich variety of gifts and their long years of experience, were soon involved in the evangelical life of the city.

The doctor served on the board of directors of a number of societies: the Scottish Reformation Society, the Bible Society of Scotland and the Edinburgh Medical Mission. In all these his contribution was of great value, especially in the case of the Edinburgh Medical Mission. For long years the society had been in touch with him, notably when he was imprisoned in Funchal and, during his periods of leave, he was always a very welcome speaker at their rallies. His example and testimony encouraged men to answer God's call to the foreign field as medical missionaries. The E.M.M. held the doctor in very high esteem: 'In his personal character, in his attainments and skill, Dr Kalley was a model of what the medical missionary ought to be, while the remarkable success which attended his "labour of love and work of faith" is a most striking illustration of what a Christian physician may do as an evangelist, ever boldly maintaining the honour of his divine Master's cause, and ready to suffer, if need be, for it.'

Memorable conversations

It was in the home, however, that the Kalleys made their most valuable contribution to the work in Edinburgh. They kept open house and as a hostess Mrs Kalley excelled. Students were especially attracted and Saturday night would find the drawing room crowded with young folk. Conversation flowed freely and was always channelled effortlessly into spiritual matters. Although Mrs Kalley's magnetic personality captivated most attention at these homely gatherings, the doctor always had a special part to play. Mrs Kalley wrote, 'On our happy Saturday evenings at Campo Verde many a dear young friend loved to get away to the corner near my husband's chair, and I doubt not that the angels, and the Lord of the angels, loved to hear those quiet, unforgotten conversations. One-by-one, heart-to-heart, face-to-face, was his special method of doing his Master's work, though by no means the only one.' She added: 'I was often amazed at the way in which his words, very casual words, we might have called them, were remembered and recalled after many years.' A case in point well illustrates that fact.

In a letter to the E.M.M. Dr Kalley wrote: 'I passed a summer in the Lebanon (1852) and while there devoted four or five hours daily to seeing the sick, and supplying them with medicines: many came from great distances. I seldom went to the houses of my patients, but I made an exception in the case of a young man employed in a silk factory. This youth's mother suffered from dropsy for which, along with other medicines, I tapped her. Her son was present on these occasions. I left Syria soon after and did not see my patient again, neither did I hear from her son until a few weeks ago, when I received a letter, written in broken English, by one of his children. It is dated December 1st 1883, fully thirty-one years after our last interview. In it he reminds me of the operation on his mother, and then adds: "Your speaking to me was always of the gospel. I listened to your words not because I believed you, but that you should attend my mother." He tells of his marriage, of his being a Greek priest, of acting as such "with pleasure for eight years". From the ninth to the seventeenth year of his priesthood, he says, "Your sermons began to grow in my heart." Then, conscience obliged him to give up the priesthood; he began meetings for spiritual worship in his own house; he was much persecuted, but the Lord was with him. He has now been a Protestant teacher for ten years. Forty meet in his house for worship and twelve are communicants. He writes: "Your words which were buried in my heart for many years, then they grew, and became by God's grace, a large tree which flourishes and will continue to bring forth fruit by the power of God." He adds: "You must know that when I heard that you were still alive, my joy was as Joseph's joy when he heard that his father was still alive: but oh! where shall I bring the chariots from to send for you?"'

In her memoirs, Mrs Kalley wrote, 'I often wonder whether other saints of God have such holy dreams as my dear husband often had ... often I awoke to find him ready, overflowing with some blessed thought of God ... very often he would go on with these heavenly things till I had to recall him to the coming earthly duties of the day ... feeling very earthly myself as I did it. But there was nothing in the least stilted in all this; only one felt that his loving lowly heart really dwelt among the things of God and rejoiced in them exceedingly.' 'My dear husband's frequent petition – "May we know God, as if it were seeing him." I think that I must have heard him in private and family prayers, and public ones, too, ask this of his Lord some thousand times, and always with the same tones of deep and holy awe.'

The doctor and the Established Church

Contrary to his own expectations on his return to Edinburgh, Dr Kalley remained a member of the established Church of Scotland. In her *Recollections in Memoriam*, Mrs Kalley wrote, 'When my husband was converted (1834/35) it was with the Established Church that he was connected. It was some of the ministers and elders of that church who condemned him for intruding into a work for which he had no right when, as a young Christian doctor, he assembled the poor and ignorant to explain the Scriptures to them ... He also received help from ministers of that church, most of whom, however, left the Establishment at the Disruption. At that time (1843), though warmly sympathizing with the movement, he did not join the Free Church, being so much absorbed by work in Madeira to have leisure for even that: and therefore, he really belonged to the Established Church to the end. For, when we left Brazil in 1876, we found the Free Church in a very different position to that which it occupied in earlier years. The discussion of the Robertson Smith case was in progress, and though the result showed that the majority of Free Church leaders were not yet ready to endorse rationalistic and infidel views, my dear husband saw enough to deter him from formally uniting himself with it. He told his decision to our dear friend, Dr Horatius Bonar, whose comment was, "You were quite right," for he, too, mourned the marked downward tendency of the church he had loved and served so well.'

The question of baptism

In Brazil the question has been asked and debated, did Dr Kalley or his wife (he a Presbyterian and she a Congregationalist) ever seek rebaptism in accordance with the custom of believers' baptism which they established in the church in Brazil? In 1837, in answer to a questionnaire sent to him by the L.M.S., he wrote regarding baptism: 'I consider this ordinance most fearfully prostituted. I have endeavoured in my place to awaken ministers and elders and people to the unspeakable dangers incurred by this and other abuses. I am quite satisfied that infants should be baptized, but only infants of such as do solemnly profess Christ and live lives becoming the gospel.' Years later, after his experiences as a missionary in Madeira and Brazil, his views on infant baptism underwent a change. In a letter he explained his position: ' The prerequisites for baptism are: (a) the gospel message must be clearly understood; (b) the heart must be open to receive that message' , and his conclusion was that these prerequisites of faith and joy are 'null and void in the case of a child'!

In correspondence with his wife's uncle John Morley, of Brethren persuasion, he clarifies further his position. Baptism with water is symbolic of baptism with the Holy Spirit, and the former without the latter is meaningless, a mere ritual. It certainly cannot save, but is a public confession of a radical change wrought by salvation. On the basis of the Lord's death the believer is united to him, and becomes one with him through the Holy Spirit, and he concludes that the New Testament does not establish any form which is 'unique, special, obligatory or universal'. He himself favoured baptism by sprinkling as the symbol nearest to baptism with the Holy Spirit, and this was established as customary in the churches he founded in Brazil.

He respected the practices of other denominations, whether paedobaptist or immersionist: to him the form of baptism was not of prime importance. There is no evidence that either he or his wife ever sought rebaptism by aspersion, and certainly not by immersion.

25.
News from Brazil

Involved as they were in the spiritual side of life in Edinburgh, the Kalleys' primary concern continued to be that of the work they had established abroad. Correspondence flowed between them and the churches in Rio de Janeiro and Recife and, in a lesser degree, with Illinois, Madeira and Portugal. Dr Kalley spent much of his time writing lengthy pastoral letters to the churches in Brazil.

Such letters became more numerous when the Rev. Santos found himself increasingly drawn into the controversy with the Plymouth Brethren on points of doctrine and church polity. The life of the church was seriously disrupted, many of the members, followers of Richard Holden, adhering to the new doctrines and seeking assiduously to proselytize those faithful to the truths they had learned from Dr Kalley. The doctor wrote eight lengthy epistles warning the believers in Rio and Recife of the dangers of accepting 'Darbyism', with its anti-pastoral bias and its emphasis on the individual to the detriment of the concept of the church. Dr Kalley considered the matter to be so urgent that he invited his friend Spurgeon to come to his aid. This Mr Spurgeon readily did, and sent the Rev. Santos literature on the subject to help him stem the tide of 'P-Bism' in the Fluminense Church. The effort was successful and a number of erring church members returned to the fold, disillusioned with the practical outworking of Darby's doctrines. Even Vianna in Recife had been invited to join the *Darbistas*!

Dr Kalley explained why he did not treat of such matters through the medium of the press: 'It is only when I think that an error is being expounded that justifies a defence, that I spend time and effort to write against it. I pray that the Lord may bless what I write now, and that he may keep from error and falsehood his little flock in Rio de Janeiro.'

A pastor for Recife

One matter which weighed heavily on the doctor's mind and heart was the urgent need for more help for Recife. The two students from there, Aderito and Leônides, were making good progress in the East London Training Institute, but time would elapse before they were ready to return to Pernambuco. The Rio church was being very effectively shepherded by the Rev. Santos, but Recife stood in dire need of a teaching ministry, something which Vianna was not qualified to give. A student who had befriended Aderito, William Bowers, received a definite call from God to go to Recife. The principal of the college, Dr Grattan Guinness, gave his wholehearted endorsement, and a personal interview with Bowers convinced Dr Kalley that here was God's man to meet the need of the struggling cause in Recife. In order to help with the finances the doctor consulted the British and Foreign Bible Society, and they agreed to employ Bowers as an agent. William Bowers was duly ordained and set aside for the ministry by a group of pastors at a 'Baptist Tabernacle' in London. He registered his ordination document with the Brazilian Consulate, and was thus officially recognized as a clergyman, with the right to conduct weddings, funerals and any other pastoral duties that required endorsement by the civil authorities.

Bowers sailed for Pernambuco, arriving there on 14 March 1878. A week later he was duly elected pastor of the Pernambucana Church. On Sunday he preached at the morning service and, for a beginner, spoke Portuguese very well. He wrote to Dr Kalley enthusiastically: he had been very well received by the church; he was enjoying life in the city; in spite of an epidemic of fever prevalent at the time, he was in excellent health. In a letter to Dr Kalley, Vianna's wife takes up the story: 'On the 28th [March] Mr Bowers was sitting in the shade in the garden, contentedly munching biscuits as he conversed with my husband. As he sat there I took him the remainder of church books which should be in his keeping. The following day he turned up at our house again, *en route* for the church. He was perfectly well. Next day he was taken ill, but my husband only heard of it a day later. My husband himself had been ill and was still laid up in bed, but he immediately dressed and went to see Bowers. He found him in high fever, and straight away sent for a doctor. The doctor declared that Bowers was suffering from the dreaded yellow fever, and added that in all probability he would not recover, since he was so new to the country.

'We begged the doctor to do everything possible for Mr Bowers, as though he were a son. The doctor began treatment right away, and the following day called two of his colleagues to study the case with him. All agreed that the right treatment was being given, but that the outlook was grave. During the day my husband stayed with him and at night, Mr Smith, the Presbyterian missionary. On the 2nd April at 10 o'clock at night they called my husband. He saw that the end was near, and at two in the morning as my husband knelt at the bedside and prayed, our good friend passed away. At four o'clock that afternoon we carried him to his grave.'

Since the Catholic Church had not discovered a ceremony whereby they could 'unconsecrate' a corner in the cemetery where non-Catholics might be laid to rest according to government legislation, the so-called heretic was refused burial in 'consecrated' ground. Lovingly and sorrowfully the members of the church carried his mortal remains to an enclosure outside the cemetery walls where criminals and suicides were buried. To safeguard the grave from any form of desecration the church bought the plot and erected a memorial stone – a thing unheard of in the 'cemetery of the hung ones'. The pathos and agony of the whole incident are reflected in the detailed account of the burial recorded in the minute book of the Pernambucana Church. The grief and bewilderment of the little group, only twelve in all, knew no bounds: they were stunned. What they had seen in William Bowers endeared him to them, and their hopes for a great forward movement under his leadership appeared to be well-founded. And, now ... the Lord had given and, in less than a month, had taken away.

The death of Mr Bowers brought about a crisis of leadership in the Pernambucana Church, a matter which caused Dr Kalley grave concern. Elements in the church were dissatisfied with Vianna's leadership, and the situation became so tense that Vianna and his family abandoned the church for a while and congregated with the Presbyterians. It was a demonstration of how the independent spirit of the *nortista* manifested itself even in the church! Time is the great healer and the situation gradually returned to normal, with Vianna reinstated. The church consulted the doctor as to whether a layman could preside at the Lord's Supper. This and similar queries were constantly referred to the doctor for his ruling.

Mr Fanstone goes to Recife

When news of the tragic death of William Bowers reached the training college, another student volunteered to take his place – James Fanstone. Intellectually and spiritually he was well prepared for the task, but physically he suffered a serious defect: he was lame, the result of a fall from the topmost branches of a tree, which as a boy he had been dared to climb. Convalescence over, his leg far from healed, he had climbed the tree again to prove that he could do it! Dr Guinness highly recommended James Fanstone as of sterling character, of indomitable will and of deep spirituality. Dr Guinness knew his background too, that he had been disciplined in the hard school of experience. Orphaned at an early age he was forced to leave school and earn his own living as a cobbler, in all a good preparation for the hardships he was to endure as a missionary in Brazil. Dr Kalley invited the young man to Edinburgh and was greatly impressed. He found him to be suitable in every way to the exacting demands of work in north-east Brazil. He underwent a further complicated operation on his leg and spent five months in hospital. As a result he was 'less lame', but was still obliged to use an iron on the leg, and even to resort to crutches on occasions.

By this time Leônides had completed his course and was ready to return to Brazil. The doctor signed a contract with the Bible Society of Scotland whereby both James Fanstone

and Leônides Francisco da Silva became their agents in
Recife. The Bible Society would give them a minimum allowance and a percentage of their sales of Scriptures. It was
barely enough to meet their basic needs, but both readily
undertook to go out in faith. They arrived in Recife in July
1879, and shortly afterwards Mr Fanstone was elected pastor
of the Pernambucana Church.

Experience was to prove that with his game leg, Mr
Fanstone was unable to cope with the constant journeyings
demanded by colportage. Recife is built on sand, and the
highways and byways were unpaved. It was difficult for able-
bodied people to trudge along, but for Mr Fanstone almost
impossible, since foot and crutch sank easily into the sand. It
was only his indomitable will that kept him mobile. The heat,
too, of Recife, situated just to the south of the equator, was
enervating, added to which custom demanded that on formal
occasions he wear a frock-coat and a tall hat! To support himself financially he taught English and must have become well-
known in the city, and as a teacher of English much sought
after, since records show that he taught the scions of wealthy
and influential families in their homes. Their knowledge of
English gained would stand that generation in good stead as
they became leaders in politics, industry and commerce.

He was essentially an independent, supporting himself, and
in no way dependent on donations from Dr Kalley or from
any missionary society. As a bachelor he lived alone, his life-
style simple, even frugal. As the Kalleys got to know him better – his independent spirit, his quiet unostentatious approach
to his missionary task, his qualities of leadership – their admiration for him grew. He was indeed a leader and he gathered
around him a band of loyal helpers whose names still strike a
cord of affection and pride in the hearts of members of the
Pernambucana Church – Andrade, Fonseca, Leônides, Jardim, Campelo. They were stalwarts, fearless and true in their
witness, fathers in the faith to many a soul; pillars in the
church of the living God. They were men so different in
character and so varied in gifts, and yet in brotherly love
together they served the Lord. Jardim had been converted in
the penal settlement on the island of Fernandes de Noronha
while serving a sentence for murder. As occasion offered he
would begin to testify to his faith in Christ in a loud voice,

wherever he found himself with a few minutes to spare – riding on the mule-drawn trams, at a street corner, in the hum and bustle of the market. The fanatical tirades of priests, the ribald comments of the crowds, the disdain and indifference of a few did not deter him. Andrade was cast in a gentler mould: courteous and polished in his manners, an employee of the Gas Company, he went from house to house reading meters and collecting the amounts due, and with a courtesy that could not be rebuffed he left the gospel message wherever opportunity offered. Through the witness of these men the gospel penetrated all strata of city life. The 200,000 inhabitants may well have echoed the cry of the Thessalonians: 'These that have turned the world upside down are come hither also.'

Death of Vianna

Reports on Vianna's extensive colportage journeys continued to reach Dr Kalley. Advancing years had taken their toll of his health, but his zeal was unabated. He persisted in his efforts to distribute the Scriptures and in doing so to form the nucleus of future congregations. He was in the state of Sergipe, to the south of Pernambuco, at a town on the banks of the River São Francisco, awaiting a boat to take him upstream and farther into the interior of the state, when he heard a voice advising him to return home immediately. He did so and found his son-in-law desperately ill with typhoid and his daughter laid low with high fever. He nursed them both back to normal health, only to suffer himself. He had a heart attack and died within a few hours.

One by one Dr Kalley lost his trusted and experienced helpers – Hewitson, Pitt, Gama and now Vianna. With the news of Vianna's death there also came reports that an American missionary recently arrived in Recife from the U.S.A. had died of yellow fever. During the next few decades Brazil was to prove for missionaries as much a 'white man's grave' as West Africa!

A new building in Rio

In Rio the church was fast outgrowing its meeting hall in the Rua das Partilhas. There were now well over 200 communicants and a still greater number of adherents. Larger premises had to be found. The pastor, Rev. Santos, ably supported by elders of the calibre of José Luiz Fernandes Braga, made long-term plans. They would purchase a building site in a central location, on one of the busier city thoroughfares, and erect a purpose-built 'temple', with seating accommodation for several hundred people, and ample space for the Sunday School. Miraculously a site became available on a main road, Rua Larga de São Joaquim, a hundred yards or so from a large open space that had always been the centre in Rio for recreation and ceremonial occasions, the Campo de Santana. With some difficulty the church managed to legalize its position and its right to own property – the intervention of one of Brazil's greatest politicians was necessary for this – and the site was duly purchased. The church appealed to Dr Kalley to help to raise funds for the project among his friends and acquaintances, and the doctor's efforts were at the same time well matched by the sacrificial giving of the congregation as a whole. For the doctor, an independent, it was a strange experience to appeal for funds – he had never done so before!

On 11 June 1885 one of the church elders, Bernardino Guilherme da Silva, wrote, 'Today the foundation stone of the new building was laid with all the formalities truly Christian [in contrast to the unscriptural formalities of the Catholics on such occasions]. Not all the church was present, only members of the building committee and the elders ... Prayer was offered, and rose to heaven as a sweet-smelling perfume, with the incense of the name of our great Redeemer, our Lord Jesus Christ. A number of people who were passing scaled the hoarding, but not one cried, '*Bíblias, Bíblias*', the popular and derogatory name for the believers. The Rev. Santos appears to mature daily in the things of God: he is worthy of the highest esteem, since he works untiringly for the good of the church and of the world.'

The inauguration of the new building took place on 4 April 1886, when the disturbances resulting from the annual three days' carnival in the city had died down. During those days, now as then, nothing of a solemn or ceremonial nature can possibly be carried through: the whole population is given over to revelry, carousing and dancing in the streets. The week before, the closing meetings of prayer and praise were celebrated in the Travessa das Partilhas, with thanksgiving to God for the blessing received by the church during the twenty-two years they had worshipped there. The opening ceremonies were well publicized by invitations and in the press. The elder, Bernardino, again wrote to the doctor: 'At the morning service three ministers occupied the platform. The service lasted from ten in the morning to one in the afternoon. We were afraid that the Rev. Santos' voice would not last out: he had so much he wanted to say. He gave a short history of the church, read the Twenty-Eight Articles of Faith to inform everyone of the doctrines of our faith, preached a sermon. God gave him special aid; he was in the pulpit for two and a half hours! The choir sang appropriate hymns, previously rehearsed in the Travessa das Partilhas; people marvelled at the quality and harmony of the voices. At half past four in the afternoon the Lord's Supper was celebrated. At night the crush was so great that every available space was occupied and people spilled over into the Sunday School rooms. The pastor presided and the preacher was Dr Gruel, minister of the Lutheran Church.'

This was the fourth location of the Fluminense Church and it would remain there until 3 May 1914, when growing demands of both church and Sunday School made a further change of premises a necessity.

The work in Recife prospers

Meanwhile, under Pastor Fanstone's able leadership the church in Recife prospered. Persecution in one form or another was an ever-present reality. Mockingly, and yet with a touch of humour, Brazilians nicknamed the missionary 'the little devil on crutches'! His congregation was drawn, without exception, from the masses of the poor and needy; to them the pastor was a shepherd and father. Death was an ever-present spectre, haunting those desperately poor homes – under-nourishment, fevers and above all, tuberculosis claimed its victims. Destitute fever patients were taken to a small island, separated from the mainland by a narrow channel, to be cared for in the 'fever hospital', a ramshackle building run by old hags, contemporaries of Mrs Gamp. Compassion moved Mr Fanstone to care for them, too. Whenever opportunity offered he would row across the channel, struggle through the deep sand, and bring some comfort and cheer to those pariahs of society. Dr Grattan Guinness was correct when he said that James Fanstone had an indomitable spirit; he had the love of Christ, too.

In January 1885, the Rev. Fanstone wrote a long letter to Dr Kalley, saying that he had been six years in Recife without ever having gone beyond its boundaries, and was now fully aware that he had to have a helper. Difficulties had arisen because there were no funds available for the upkeep of Leônides. Mr Fanstone outlined the type of man required for the task, a man with 'intellectual ability, active, zealous, a true imitator of the apostle Paul'. He suggested a plan of action. If a man could be sent out he would guarantee his support for the first six months, and during that period gather together a sufficient number of people wanting to learn English, in order to give the volunteer an income. He spoke of the pitfalls the young man would encounter, but emphasized the spiritual rewards he would receive.

It was not to be: no suitable candidate was forthcoming, and, exhausted with toil, Mr Fanstone returned to Britain for urgent treatment and, incidentally and unexpectedly, to marry. He met and wooed a Miss Elizabeth Baird from Edinburgh, a student in Doric Lodge – the women's section of Harley college. It was a case of love at first sight, and within four months they were married and on their way to Brazil, in March 1886. While in Britain Mr Fanstone spoke at Cliff College in Derbyshire, and a student there, Fitzgerald Holmes, heard the call to service in Brazil. He paid a brief visit to the Kalleys, but their silence regarding him indicates that they were not suitably impressed. Mr Holmes accepted Mr Fanstone's offer to fund the first six months of his stay in Brazil and joined the Fanstones in Recife, but only for a relatively short period. He later accepted the call to serve as chaplain to the Seaman's Mission in the port of Santos in the south. In Santos he did an excellent work, and that for long years, but that meant that the Fanstones were alone once more.

26.
Mission accomplished

Dr Kalley's health was a continued source of anxiety to his wife and friends. He knew that he suffered from a heart condition that might prove fatal at any moment. To this was added an irritating dermatitis that attacked his whole body. In times of stress letter-writing was difficult and, as ever, his wife stood by him and wrote his letters, whether to his beloved friends in Brazil and elsewhere overseas, or to the press. He was highly critical of what he called 'false analogies' propagated among students by Dr Henry Drummond (1851-1897), professor of theology at the Free Church College, Glasgow. These 'false analogies' related science to religion and called into question the authority of Scripture. To Dr Kalley such teaching was anathema and provoked him to write letters of protest to the press. It was to be his last controversy.

'This is death'

On 1 January 1888, a Sunday, he gathered the family together – his wife, Marianne Pitt and the household servants – to celebrate the Lord's Supper. He expressed the fervent hope that the Lord would come soon and so spare him having to pass through the portals of death. It was not to be. On Sunday 15th he conducted family worship both morning and evening. In the morning he chose the hymn: 'I'm not afraid to own my

Lord, or to defend his cause' and, in the evening, a Sankey hymn:

> Lone and weary, sad and dreary,
> Lord, I would thy call obey;
> Thee believing, Christ receiving,
> I would come to thee today.
> I am coming...
> Coming Lord to thee.

The following day he complained of a pain in the heart that was 'different'. It was diagnosed as asthma of the heart. The pain increased, becoming unbearable: nothing would relieve it. Next morning at seven o'clock he suffered a series of convulsions. Suddenly he exclaimed: 'Let me go! Let me go! This is death, O my beloved wife!'

The funeral took place at the Dean Cemetery, Edinburgh, on 24 January. The service was conducted by Dr Kalley's great friend, Dr Hudson Taylor, pioneer missionary to China and founder of the China Inland Mission. It was to China that Dr Kalley had felt called. He never got there, but his interest in China never waned, and one of the greatest missionaries to that country conducted the last rites for him!

Mrs Kalley wrote both to the Fluminense and the Pernambucana Churches giving them a detailed account of her husband's last days. Both churches felt the loss of their founder keenly, and in his memory they placed two commemorative plaques one on either side of the headstone, registering their thanks to God for his ministry.

Some years later the Rev. Dr Handley Moule, D.D., Bishop of Durham, wrote, 'A Scottish believer, strong, self-restrained, a characteristic son of the Presbyterian Church, the late Dr Kalley approached the end an aged man. As a veteran medical practitioner, he calmly told his wife, who told my informant, how he must expect to die suddenly, but that he hoped to give her notice. One day he laid his hand upon her arm, said the words: "Oh! my dear wife" and immediately expired. The words and the manner, said Mrs Kalley, were precisely those with which years before, during a tour they took in the Highlands, he had touched her arm, and bade her look, when suddenly a mountain view of entrancing grandeur broke upon them.'

After her husband's death, Sarah Kalley was desolate: Campo Verde became a house of mourning. No longer on a Saturday evening did the drawing-room echo with the chatter and laughter of students. The magnitude of her loss, even though tempered by the God of all consolation, overwhelmed her, and completely disrupted the normal routine of life. It could hardly be otherwise since she and her husband had been inseparable during thirty-five years; their lives and their labours had been entwined: a perfect combination, a perfect whole.

Tributes to the doctor

Tributes to the doctor poured in from all sources, as friends and associates remembered the 'good doctor', 'faithful pastor'; for many he was their father in the faith, and for others their co-worker in the Lord's service.

Perhaps extracts from an article in the May 1888 edition of the Edinburgh Medical Mission's magazine sum up the high regard in which Dr Kalley was held: 'There is no more convincing proof of the preciousness and power of an evangelical ministry than the simple record of the life-work of men, whose teaching is the outcome of the inquiry "What saith the Scriptures?" not "What thinkest thou?", the keynote of whose message is "Christ suffered for our sins, the just for the unjust, that he might bring us to God".

'Dr Kalley's memory will be long and lovingly cherished by many, as one of the earliest pioneers of modern medical missions, and as a valiant and faithful standard-bearer in the church's warfare against the enemies of the King. Many more love to remember him as a brother, beloved of the Lord, with whom they were privileged to take sweet counsel by the way. Of him it might appropriately have been said: "His delight is in the law of the Lord, and in his law doth he meditate day and night." "Thy testimonies also are my delight, and my counsellors"; "Chosen in him ... holy ... and without blame before him in love".'

Headstone
Dean Cemetery Edinburgh

Pastor Fanstone testifies: 'The private life of Dr Kalley deeply impressed the minds of Brazilian believers ... there is some mysterious charm about the life of Dr Kalley, when once it captivated, never lost its hold.' To which may be added the closing eulogy of Dr Michael Testa, in his biography *The Apostle of Madeira*: 'Few men are gifted with so much talent, with such strength of character and singleness of purpose, with such an attractive personality and with such capacity to serve others freely, as Dr Robert Reid Kalley.'

And the last word is that of the Spirit of God himself: 'Write: Blessed are the dead who die in the Lord from now on. Yes, says, the Spirit, they will rest from their labours, for their deeds will follow them.'

Epilogue (1888-1907)

For Sarah Kalley life did return to normal routine, admittedly truncated by the death of her husband. Her natural resilience, energized by her deep spirituality – her trust in the Lord and obedience to his Word – asserted itself, and she recovered something of her exuberance and verve for life.

Throughout this harrowing experience she had had the help of her faithful companion of long years, Marianne Pitt, and of her adopted son Dr João Rocha, as also of the Brazilian 'daughter' Sia, besides her wide circle of caring friends and relatives. As time elapsed they suggested that she open her home again to students, and so the Saturday night gatherings recommenced. The doctor's chair in the corner, however, was now vacant.

One overriding desire orientated her whole life, to which all else was subservient: she must continue the work she and her husband had begun. She could not resume his correspondence with the churches in Illinois, Trinidad and Madeira, but her contact with the churches in Brazil must be maintained. She had the advantage of knowing intimately both the work and the workers in Rio and in Recife. The Rev. Santos, José Fernandes Braga and Pastor Fanstone were her personal friends; she was resolved to continue as their loyal co-labourer.

The 'Help for Brazil'

Immediately after the funeral, the plight of the Brazil field had been the subject of conversation among interested friends. Even in the darkest days Brazil was not forgotten. At the time Brazil was passing through a period of tremendous upheaval, politically, socially and religiously. In 1888, Princess Isabel, in the absence of her father, Dom Pedro II, but with his approval, signed the decree liberating slaves. Both knew that it would cost them the throne. Brazil was essentially an agricultural country, and the vast plantations of sugar cane, coffee, maize, as also the extensive cattle ranches, depended wholly and entirely on slave labour, as indeed did the whole range of the country's activities. Half the population were slaves. The decree caught the nation by surprise, with little or no preparation for such an eventuality, and as a result the situation was chaotic. The great landowners were Brazil's aristocracy: many were ruined and they could not forgive their sovereign. The royal family of Bragança was doomed.

In November 1889 the republic was proclaimed and the emperor given only twenty-four hours to leave the country. He died in Paris as the year 1891 drew to a close.

With the coming of the republic, the Roman Catholic Church was also disestablished and, on paper at least, all religions were made equal and free to propagate their faith.

The time was ripe for a forward surge of the gospel. The Fluminense Church took the initiative. Under the dynamic leadership of its pastor, the Rev. Santos, and experienced laymen, a national missionary society, the Evangelistic Society of Rio de Janeiro, was formed on 8 November 1890. Their original aim was to evangelize more effectively the city and its extensive suburbs. Later the field was enlarged to include all the state of Rio de Janeiro, and at a still later date it became involved in the evangelization of Portugal. It then adopted a new name, the Evangelistic Missionary Society of Brazil and Portugal.

Back in Britain in 1892, Mr Fanstone and Mrs Kalley pondered the future of the work in Brazil. How could they cooperate more effectively with the Brazilian brethren in their gigantic task of evangelizing Brazil? After consultation with interested friends, they founded a mission, 'the Help for Brazil'. Mr Fanstone was appointed director, Mrs Kalley secretary, and members of the governing council chosen: Rev. Gould of Edinburgh, Dr Grattan Guinness of Harley College, Mr and Mrs Hind-Smith (she was a sister of Mrs Kalley) of Exeter Hall. Dr Hudson Taylor of the China Inland Mission proved a wise and kindly adviser to the new mission. The Kalley set-up was unique in the history of missions. Brazilians first founded their own missionary society, and then the 'foreign' mission was brought into existence to co-operate with the national mission already founded! The national mission gladly welcomed the foreign mission and the two worked happily together, co-ordinating their efforts and avoiding overlapping. They did not merge, but each kept its own identity and was responsible to choose its own missionaries and to support them.

Mrs Kalley was indefatigable in the service of the mission. She personally, with Mr Fanstone, vetted missionary candidates, and what a crop of able missionaries the 1890s yielded: – men and women whose names are revered in the history of the Kalley churches, and who suffered persecution in spite of the status given to Protestant churches in the new constitution.

All these happenings – the comings and goings of missionaries, the progress of the work, the difficulties and dangers faced – Mrs Kalley recorded in a paper she edited, called the *Occasional Paper*. She demonstrated her skill as a writer, journalist and editor, by accomplishing the impossible: she correlated the jigsaw of facts in such a way that she always gave a complete picture of the field. The sequences are co-ordinated in such a way that it is possible to trace the development of any happening.

Death of Mrs Kalley

For Mrs Kalley the end came in 1907 at her home in Edinburgh. By one of those strange coincidences that do occur, the Rev. Santos was in Britain at the time and was able to take part in the funeral service. To quote from a letter written by Sia Kalley from Campo Verde on 12 August 1907, 'Mrs Kalley's last illness commenced in November the previous year, and in the early stages was accompanied by a good deal of suffering. Hope of recovery did not diminish until the last few weeks. Again and again, after accessions of illness, unexpected rallies ensued, and wonderful vitality characterized even the last fortnight. But her work was done and in his own good time, the Lord whom she had served took her home on the 8th instant, and today she was laid to rest beside her dear husband in the Dean Cemetery. At her own request the words: "Heirs together of the grace of life" will be inscribed on the stone that marks the spot.'

Her loss was deeply mourned. Letters written from Britain and Brazil reveal the great esteem in which she was held, and how great had been her influence on so many. Even the daily press in Rio de Janeiro published two obituary columns praising her for her service to Brazil – something unique, for a Protestant missionary to be so honoured! Among other things the article acknowledged her pioneer efforts to compose hymns, adapt them to music and, above all, teach the common people to sing them. It concluded by saying that her memory would be revered down through the years, perhaps through the centuries, because of her hymns.

Here are a few quotations from the numerous letters received by Miss Sia Kalley.

'Well do I remember the happy times at Campo Verde in 1880-84, when a student in Edinburgh, and look back on those social evenings with great joy at the home of our "Edinburgh mother".

'She could have no idea what an influence for good she always had on me, and, I believe, on all who came into contact with her.'

'She never failed, even in the darkest hour, in a certain measure of lightsome humour, which would not fail to diminish the gloom.'

'The sad tidings have come – sad to many – to those who knew and dearly loved Mrs Kalley here; to students who will ever venerate her; to those who laboured under her inspiration in Brazil; to her spiritual children in both hemispheres … she was so brimful of life,… so warm-hearted, so rich in piety and good works.'

'So great was the personal influence exerted by Dr and Mrs Kalley over the lives of Brazilian Christians that the whole subsequent history of the *Igrejas Evangélicas* has been moulded and directed by it. These churches do not coincide with any particular sect in Britain, but have a character peculiarly their own. They stand for the old Puritan faith... the hymns used were written and translated generally by Dr and Mrs Kalley themselves. The high regard, amounting to veneration, of the older members of the churches who knew Dr and Mrs Kally personally is really astounding, and this veneration has been handed down to the younger members of the churches in a remarkable degree, so that these names are household words, like Wesley in England.'

And, from the council of the Help for Brazil came a brief statement reflecting the trial that had overtaken it in the removal of Mrs Kalley, and the new sense of responsibility with which it resolved to continue the work begun: 'Mrs Kalley was the soul of the council. It was around her that the members gathered. The intensity of her interest in everything bearing upon the spiritual welfare of Brazil, the enthusiasm with which she devoted herself to the maintenance and extension of the mission she was instrumental in founding, and the success with which she laboured to infuse her own self-sacrificing zeal into the wide circle of her relations and friends, were a constant inspiration and stimulus to her advisers and fellow-workers in the council ... They earnestly hope, therefore, that the memory of her consecration of so large a part of her time and means to the evangelization of Brazil will constrain all who knew her, whether with that high admiration and affection which intimacy with her inspired, or without the privilege of close association, to help to continue the much-needed work that lay so near her heart, with new liberality and regularity.'

And now?

In Madeira there still exist four churches that owe their existence to Dr Kalley's ministry. They are the Presbyterian Churches in Funchal, Louro (a suburb of Funchal), Machico and Ribeira Brava. They form part of the Presbyterian Synod in Lisbon. At the time of writing they have one minister, a Brazilian. They have no links with the Free Church of Scotland.

In Illinois the churches in Jacksonville and Springfield have merged into the Presbyterian Church in the U.S.A. They no longer retain their Portuguese identity.

In Brazil the Kalley churches have expanded into the *União das Igrejas Evangélicas Congregacionais do Brasil,* numbering 700 in all. Although the majority are in the Rio - Pernambuco areas, the union has churches in most of the states of Brazil.

In Britain the Help for Brazil was incorporated in 1913 in the newly formed Evangelical Union of South America, some of whose missionaries still serve the Congregational churches in Brazil in specialized ministries, principally, theological education.

The Fluminense Church in Rio de Janeiro continues to maintain the *Missão Evangelizadora do Brasil e Portugal.* This mission, at the turn of the century, founded a dozen churches in Portugal, the majority of which now form part of the Presbyterian Synod of Lisbon. The remainder, in Ponte de Sor, Lisbon and Paio Pires, have united to form the *União das Igrejas Evangélicas Congregacionais do Portugal.* The *Missão Evangelizadora* still retains its interest in these churches, as does, more recently, the British Evangelical Fellowship of Congregational Churches.

Appendix I

Declaration made by the first group of Madeirans transported from Trinidad to New York
August 1848

We, the undersigned, all natives of Madeira, were born and educated in the Roman Catholic Church. It was ever our custom to attend mass, confession of sins, and take part in the various ceremonies, fasts and festivals of the Catholic Church. We did not know any other form of worship, since none of us had either seen or heard the Word of God as yet. We did not know that a book called the Bible existed, in which the story of Jesus and the apostles is told, until Dr Kalley came to Madeira. Reading the Bible that he gave us we learnt from the very first reading of it that we can only be saved by the blood of Jesus, and not by masses, penitences and purgatory. We learned that neither the Virgin nor the saints are our mediators, because there is only one mediator between God and men, Christ Jesus. When we began to rejoice in Christ Jesus as our mediator and to read the Scriptures with joy, we were prohibited from reading the Bible by the Catholic Church and by the state. The priests began to confiscate our Bibles and to burn them. Many readers of the Bible were thrown into prison. Some have been in jail for two years and some for three. We have been evicted from our homes and our lands, sleeping rough in caves and wandering over the mountains, because we read the Word of God and because we wish to live according to its precepts, and for no other reason. We were compelled by the priests and by the State Governor to flee the country and leave behind all we

possessed – houses, lands, goods. We are completely destitute and in a foreign country. As to the truth of these state-
ments we are prepared to testify before the whole world.'

(Signed by sixty Madeirans of all ages)

Appendix II

'How frequently does the true follower of the Lord Jesus Christ see and hear of good fields, and hopeful centres of gospel witness and patient endeavour to lead precious souls into the fold of Christ, becoming in the course of a few years of happy and prosperous existence, invaded, disturbed, disorganized and destroyed by the operation of subtle influences of a pseudo-religious character, social and political doctrines that oppose the sublime, enlightening and purifying power of the Word of God? The true church of Jesus Christ is by its regenerated nature essentially an exclusive body; it is in the world but not of the world. But the so-called Christian church, in all its sub-divisions, is subject to the attacks of the power that transforms himself into an "angel of light", but who is in reality a "raging lion seeking to devour". We have to wait, therefore, for the proposed new heavens and new earth where there will be no more curse, because the adversary shall be cast out for evermore.'

Gathered thoughts when troubles and dissensions plagued the Kalley Churches, principally in Illinois in 1854.

Appendix III

Press Release
November 1976
Brazilians honour first pioneer

An interesting ceremony took place at the Dean Cemetery in Edinburgh last month when a floral tribute was laid on the grave of Dr Robert Reid Kalley (first Protestant missionary to Brazil) on behalf of the Order of Protestant Ministers in Brazil and of the forty-four-man delegation from that country to the Eleventh World Pentecostal Congress. In a short discourse, prepared by the delegates, allusion was made to the fact that Dr Kalley together with his wife, Mrs Sarah Kalley, had been the founder and organizer of the first Sunday School in Brazil in the town of Petropolis on the 15th August 1855.

The citation continued: 'Dr Kalley was the medical attendant of the Emperor, D. Pedro II, and in fulfilling his noble profession, also spread the precious seed in Rio de Janeiro (the then-capital of the empire) Petropolis and other states of the country. He suffered persecutions by the Roman clergy but the seed had fallen in good ground and it grew, producing fruit in abundance, a crop which we are still reaping. A good and faithful servant, he knew how to do business with the talents which had been given him by his Lord and for this his works do follow him. Dr Kalley was a doctor but above all else, a missionary.'

Originally, the delegation had planned to visit the grave of the renowned pioneer and to do honour to his memory, but it was discovered that this was not practicable by reason of time and distance since the Congress was held in London.

The Rev. R.G. Grant, General Secretary of the EUSA, who was currently in the United Kingdom, was therefore invited to represent the Brazilian party and ministers and there was a certain appropriateness in this since the EUSA has close historical links with Dr and Mrs Kalley.

After Mr Grant, who has been resident in Brazil since 1954, had read the discourse in English and in Portuguese and had laid the wreath sent by the Brazilian representatives, Psalm 67 was read and a prayer of gratitude offered by Mr Stuart J. Harrison, of the EUSA and the National Bible Society of Scotland, himself a missionary to South America for twenty years. Among the number who attended was Miss C.F. Norrie, M.B.E., who had been closely and continually associated with the work in South America since 1912.

The simple but moving ceremony concluded as Mr Grant, on behalf of the Brazilian contingent, thanked those present for their participation.

Select bibliography

The following books were lent by the Canning Library, London:
English Church in Madeira, The, H.A. Newall, Oxford University Press.
Impressions of Madeira in the past, Luiz de Santos Mello & Susan E. Farrow, English Bookshop.
O Rio como é, uma vez e nunca mais, D. Schlichthorst.

The following were made available by courtesy of the Fluminense Church Library, Rio de Janeiro:
Collated facts, in chronological order, of the Kalleys' day-to-day life, João Rocha, Fluminense Library.
Escbóço Histórico da Escola Domínical da Igreja Fluminense, 1855-1932.
Lembranças do Passado, João Rocha, ed. Ismael da Silva Jr, vols I-IV.
Os Calvinistas na Madeira 1839-1856, João Fernandes da Rocha.
Volumous correspondence and diaries of Dr and Mrs Kalley, Fluminense Library.

Books and papers from other sources, including the author's own library:
A Epopéia da Ilha de Madeira, Manoel Porto Filho.
Edinburgh Medical Mission, *Quarterly Paper*, May 1888.
Herois da Fé Congregacional, vol. I, Robert Reid Kalley, vol. II. João Manoel Gonçalves Santos & Filomena Araujo dos Santos.
Madeira or the Spirit of the Antichrist, J. Roddam Tate, 1846.
O Apóstolo da Madeira, Michael P. Testa, (trans. Manuel Campos), Igreja Evangélica Presbiteriana do Portugal.
Salmos e Hinos, Henriqueta Rosa Fernandes Braga.
Seitas Protestantes de Pernambuco, Vicente Ferrer de Barros Wanderley de Araujo, Jornal do Recife.
Short Statement of Dr Kalley's Case, A, Robert R. Kalley
Um Judeu Errante no Brasil: Solomon Guinsberg, Casa Publicadora Batista.
Vision of Eden, A, Marianne North.

Index

Index

Index